Praise for the author

Erma Ranieri, Commissioner for Public Sector Employment: *"I am responsible for the largest employer in SA and so I know how important culture and leadership are in creating lasting and quality outcomes for the community. I'm thrilled that Michelle is sharing her years of experience and her extensive knowledge of culture in this book."*

Sharyn Boer, CEO, Meals on Wheels SA: *"Our social enterprise serves an important section of our community and I want the best outcomes for them. That's why, with Michelle's help, we have focused so strongly on creating a highly collaborative and customer-centric culture. Michelle's understanding of what you need to do to create the kind of culture you need for your customer, and her ability to communicate this understanding is excellent, and it's fantastic she's sharing it in this book. I know for purpose and commercial business leaders will benefit from Michelle's experience and knowledge."*

Carly Thompson-Barry, Managing Director and Founder Sass Collective: *"Through the Sass Collective, I work with entrepreneurs and female change makers who are working hard to create businesses that deliver results and that their customers and employees love. One thing I know for sure is that business culture and leadership ability is critical to their success. Michelle shared her expertise in these areas with participants at our recent Sass Summit. Our participants valued her presentation and I'm thrilled that she is sharing it more broadly through her new book."*

Leko Novakovic, Managing Director and Founder, Novatech Creative Event Technology: *"Novatech is a fast-moving company serving customers internationally. We work in a highly competitive market and have a strong focus on quality, and that's why we focus so much on leadership and culture. With Michelle's help we identified what our strengths and opportunities were, and she has helped us to create a way to fix the gaps. She also helped us to bring our people along for the journey. I know other business owners will benefit from Michelle's ability to dissect problems, and to help design a culture that works for their customers and teams."*

Kym Williams, Entrepreneur and Managing Director BRS: *"I had the pleasure of working with Michelle on several engagements in relation to leadership, culture and business improvement. Michelle is very passionate around these key initiatives and works very proactively to make positive changes. Michelle's persistence combined with her vast experience will ensure that changes identified and worked through in a range of people and culture initiatives, will be implemented successfully."*

Tyson O'Connell, General Manager Corporate Services, AG Security Group: *"Michelle is a very talented professional with many years of experience developing senior executive leaders. Michelle's mentoring, coaching, training and leadership capabilities are outstanding, further her passionate pursuit for growing and supporting emerging leaders is infectious. Her expertise in leadership development and branding, in addition to organizational culture and talent management is highly valued. I highly recommend Michelle's capabilities, leadership and value."*

Jasmin Riecke, Executive Leader, People and Communication, ReturnToWork SA: *"Michelle considers issues broadly and is able to present a compelling business case and drive outcomes. She's a pleasure to work with."*

Mike Schwarzer, Performance Strategist and Modeller: *"Michelle is a visionary, a strategic thinker and as such, courageous in taking risks and challenging the status quo. In addition, she has the ability to make things happen through people. She has the ability to connect with the people at the coalface as well as at senior level. Her energy is infectious. Michelle is a true people's person yet doesn't suffer fools gladly."*

Skye Browne, Senior Coordinator Organizational Wellbeing, Adelaide City Council: *"Michelle saw a capability in me that I never knew existed and not only did she make me see it too, but her exceptional leadership, coaching and mentoring skills have helped me harness and build on my capabilities and help achieve some major milestones for my organization. Michelle is highly motivated, and her self-belief is infectious across a team and an organization. She is an exceptional presenter and I always found her training and presentations to be well structured and exciting."*

Nicole Newton, Manager, People and Culture, City of Payneham Norwood St Peters: *"I worked with Michelle for a number of years in organizational development, learning and development and culture management. Her ideas and enthusiasm are inspiring and fun. Her drive to challenge the status quo resulted in innovative and exciting programming. Feedback from participants indicated the leadership programming and her personal mentoring was highly valued, engaging and supported them in career development. I often draw on our 'philosopher's walks' to inspire solutions in my work."*

Sandhya Burton, Community Engagement Librarian, City of Monash: *"From Michelle I learnt great strategies and processes that previously had never come easily to me, and four years on I can still see aspects of my own leadership that were influenced by her methods and examples. Michelle is a person and a business woman who others can easily look up to, and I am certain that many other people will also feel that she has left a lasting impression on them as well."*

CULTURE INC.

GLOBAL
PUBLISHING
GROUP

Global Publishing Group
Australia • New Zealand • Singapore • America • London

CULTURE INC.

INC.

International No. 1 Best Seller

Create a Business That Delivers Results and People Love

MICHELLE T HOLLAND

First Edition 2018

National Library of Australia
Cataloguing-in-Publication entry:

Michelle Holland
Culture Inc. Create a Business That Delivers Results and People Love

1st ed.
ISBN: 9781925288681 (pbk.)

A catalogue record for this book is available from the National Library of Australia

Published by Global Publishing Group
PO Box 517 Mt Evelyn, Victoria 3796 Australia
Email Info@GlobalPublishingGroup.com.au

For further information about orders:
Phone: +61 3 9739 4686 or Fax +61 3 8648 6871

This book is dedicated to my fellow culture warriors, who work hard to create work and school environments where people feel safe, valued and engaged. You are true leaders. There are times where working on culture change is thankless and exhausting. I want to thank you. Without your work there are many people who would not feel valued, or safe.

And to you. To be brave enough to pick up this book and admit that your culture isn't as great as you'd like takes courage and awareness. You have started. The journey of a thousand miles starts with the first step.

Carry on culture warrior!

Michelle T Holland

Acknowledgements

Firstly, I want to acknowledge my children, Connor and Riley. They are my biggest fans and provide me with so much love and support that my heart overflows. I want to thank them for giving me the energy, strength and purpose to keep going, even when I don't want to. They are smart, brave and fun and make me proud every day. Love you guys!

A special thank you to Riley who created the illustrations in this book. I am so happy to have you involved in the creative process.

My mum, dad, brother Scott and sister-in-law Emma, and my partner Pete who remain a consistent source of inspiration and love. My incredible niece Paige and my sweet little nephew Arlo are always in my heart.

Without my family, friends and colleagues supporting me along the way I couldn't write, do my work, and support my clients. They are always there with a gentle word of encouragement or a swift kick up the bum when I need it.

The strength that I receive from the amazing women that I am lucky to call my friends is something that I credit with keeping my head above water when I feel like I'm drowning. Joanne and Megan, you have stayed with me the longest, are a constant source of strength, and a shoulder to lean on when I need it. The 'female mafia' Jane, Tami, Karen and Kate, how could I have gotten through the culture challenges at 'you know where' without you? Thanks for the laughs, friendship and the generous supply of wine.

To my mentors and the people who have inspired me throughout my career, I thank you. Specifically, Erma Ranieri for being my mentor and helping me start this culture warrior journey. Rum Charles for coming into my life and providing encouragement just when I was about to give up. Andrew O'Keeffe for your wisdom, guidance and inspiration early in my consulting career. JK Rowling for showing me that you can achieve the seemly impossible dream and do it with grace and humor. Oprah Winfrey for years of challenging my mindset, particularly in my young years. Brené Brown for helping me see that you can be vulnerable and still a strong independent woman, and to Anna Doecke for helping me truly understand Brené's wisdom fully. Simon Sinek, Daniel Pink, Ed Catmull, Tony Hsieh, Elizabeth Gilbert, and Wayne Dyer for sending your sage ideas and words out into the world so I could learn and grow from them.

To my grandparents, you are forever in my heart and I'm grateful that I had you to inspire me during my life and are now looking after me in your afterlife.

I want to acknowledge my amazing clients. I've learnt so much from working with you and through your dedication, trials and errors, and successes, I've been able to share the learnings in this book to help others. You are working hard to create better businesses. It's tough and takes energy, but creating a business that you can be proud of and your people love makes it worthwhile. I'm thrilled to be part of your journey. I have kept all names out of the book to protect the innocent... and the not so innocent.

And to the many culture warriors that have (and continue to) contributed to my life in so many ways, Mike, Nicole, Skye, Rajan, Julie, Vashti, Jo, Kathryn, Kylie, Marisa, Matt, Jude, Frank, Tracy, Kerry, Amanda, Fi, Katie and Daniel, to name a few, you guys are making a difference. Carry on culture warriors!

Bonus Offer

Do you want to know how you and your people are contributing to the culture? Are they helping or hindering?

Because of your investment in this book I'm offering you a free gift.

Download the "SynergyIQ Culture Archetypes" video series and PDF for free. This video and PDF provides more information about the Archetypes discussed in this book. These Archetypes provides you with a way of creating change and ensuring that the people in your business are helpers and don't hinder your change efforts.

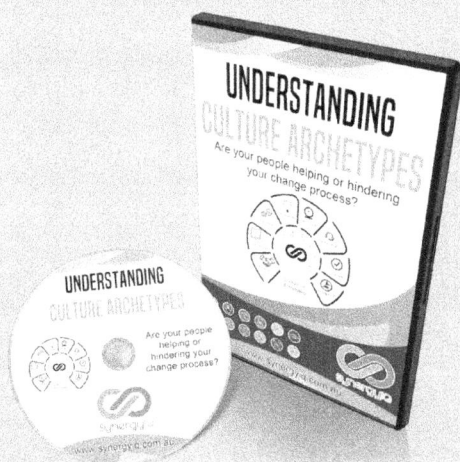

DOWNLOAD NOW AT

http://synergyiq.com.au/bookbonuses/

Contents

Preface by Author

As an immigrant in a new country it became obvious that I didn't belong. I said funny things, in a funny accent. I wore strange clothes because I didn't understand the trends. I wasn't familiar with the TV shows they spoke of, or the sports teams they cared about. I was a bookworm, so I wanted to talk about things like the environment and the world rather than the latest starlet's new handbag. I had traveled around the world so I wanted to talk about exploring and adventures, and this made me an oddity. In a school where everyone was second generation white Australian, other than the one Aboriginal girl and one Aboriginal boy, I was a prime target for bullying. I was strange. I was weird.

I eventually found ways to combat the bullies by keeping my mouth shut and trying to blend in. I spent the first few years in this new country working desperately hard to *not* be me. Being me meant pain and loneliness and who wants that when you are ten years old?

All through school I stood out when I spoke. So I stopped speaking. I would hide in plain sight with hope that I'd avoid the name calling, the poorly executed mimicking of my accent and the ostracism. I learnt to hide in plain sight. When I think back to that time I can't help but wonder how the Aboriginal kids fared. Or the kids from the Asian families who eventually moved to the area. I could hide by staying silent. They could not. But at that time I was too worried about how I was going to survive high school to think about helping them.

When I talk to people about their school years they tend to come from one of three camps. The popular ones who had lots of friends and enjoyed school, the middle group who for them school was just an activity that they did when they were young, and the people like me. The misfits, the ones who had a quality that made them different from the pack... the targets of bullies.

The mistake you will make is assuming that the people who bullied me came from the popular crowd, this is true but they also came from the other groups too. The thing that seems to bond children the most is picking on someone who they believe is different and therefore not as valuable. I have two children now, and we talk about bullying at school. Even though I have worked hard to build their self-esteem, they compare themselves to others and just want to fit in. Bullying and bigotry is still happening 30 years after my experience… we know so much more about the lasting and devastating effects of bullying and yet it appears we aren't teaching acceptance of difference. Instead many parents teach their kids to fit in whatever the cost, and sadly some still teach bigotry, avoidance and rejection.

Fast forward a few years to my first experiences in the workplace. By this time I'd mastered the art of hiding in plain sight. My routine was perfected, my accent modified after countless hours practicing to speak 'Australian'… my mum often recounts my nightly exercises…. naaooowaaa, naaooowaaa, naaaooowaa …. perfecting an Australian 'no' was my goal.

Finally, outside of the school environment I discovered something I could be valued for, my work ethic. I didn't have to work at fitting in as much because I had a job to do and the managers were keen on keeping people really busy. I liked busy. Busy was safety to me. It meant that people stayed away and I could conquer my tasks in silence. I still like busy. The interactions I had helping customers were short enough to hide my accent but long enough to feel valuable to them. I could have short but positive interactions with the other employees within the 20 minute lunch break. It was the perfect place to hide, while still being me.

Other than my family home, work was the first place that I felt valued and at peace. I couldn't wait to do it full time and permanently hide from the schoolyard bullies.

How silly I was with that prediction. I discovered almost immediately that to get by at work, you had to fit in, and the schoolyard bullies were allowed to rule in many workplaces. I still didn't understand the football teams, but I learnt a few names of footballers and the teams to get by. I still didn't speak the same as them, but I'd learnt to add a few 'mates' and 'crikeys' to my repertoire to pass for Australian in short conversations.

I made friends with people and tried to act as they did, even when it felt uncomfortable. I never understood why people wanted to talk about others in a nasty way, but I did it. To fit in. "Did you see what she was wearing?" we'd say in the lunchroom. I didn't understand why it matter what 'she' wore, and I'd feel awful for the rest of the day, but I'd say it.

I eventually became a HR Manager. I think my experiences with bullying and not feeling valued led me here. I wanted to be a lawyer when I was younger but didn't get the grades to get in to the course. I thought in HR I could help the downtrodden and that's where I headed.

But even there I found I stood out as strange. I wasn't as 'corporate polished' as others in HR. I didn't wear the designer shoes or dresses. I didn't have the ability to do an up style. I didn't go straight to university after private school. I didn't want to act like the business etiquette police officer. Again, I didn't fit.

That's when I created my disguise. My 'HR Manager Mask' I call it. I'd pop it on in the morning with a deep breath and a fancy suit, and I'd head out the door ready to be 'HR'. I wore that mask for ten years. Eventually it became hard to take off. It got stuck and even when I was with my family and friends I wore it.

I was out to dinner with a group of work friends one night. One of the women was telling a story about an encounter she'd had at work. Clearly poker is not my game because my friend looked at me and said, "You're being HR aren't you? I can see you're not enjoying this night." How astute she was. What she didn't know was how often I didn't enjoy something because I was being 'HR'. I wore the mask so often it became who I was. Which worked for my endeavor to fit in at work, and it was great for my career progression, but effected my ability to feel valued for being me.

There are countless stories I could share about being treated badly at work or witnessing awful behavior and situations of which even the worst of the school bullies would be ashamed. But I'll save them for another time.

I do want to tell you about what happened when I finally took off the mask.

For ten years I was safe. Safe under the mask. I fit in. I didn't rock the boat, although those that knew me in those years would tell you I did. They didn't know how much I was holding back.

In my last year of full time employment I did a program called 'Governor's Leadership Foundation' or GLF for short. It was the premier leadership program of the year and they only accepted people they believed were true leaders.

I applied and after my interview, I received feedback that shook me. They told me that they weren't going to accept me because I appeared too 'corporate' and didn't stand out as an individual enough.

I wanted to scream. "Are you kidding? I've spent my whole life working damn hard to fit in so that I was out of the way of the pain of rejection and bullying. Now I'm being rejected for fitting in? What is going on universe?!?!?"

Thankfully I was given a second chance to take off the mask and show them who I was. And they accepted me for being me. You have no idea what that felt like. I thought about that young Canadian girl who stopped speaking in school. How all she wanted was to be accepted for who she was. Finally I found my place.

Throughout that year I practised more at being me. The people in the course appreciated it and so I eventually took off the mask and threw it away.

Unfortunately my place of employment didn't appreciate it as much. They wanted the mask-wearing Michelle. The one that fit in and didn't rock the boat. But I knew to be happy, proper happy, I'd have to just be me.

After a number of months of disappointing treatment by people I trusted in that business I left. I knew that I couldn't be in another job because I couldn't go through the pain of either being me and being bullied, or the pain of trying to wear that mask again. It just didn't fit anymore.

That's when I started my business. Through soul searching and writing, I created a new me and a new business. I work with business leaders to create great workplaces. I help them to challenge the status quo, improve business systems and culture, and create workplaces that deliver holistic results that people love.

I love my work. The reason I do it is because I don't want anyone to experience the mask-wearing, 'pretending to be someone you're not' pain I experienced throughout my life. My core mission is to create businesses that have environments where people feel safe and valued. It's what keeps me going when things are tough. My mission is what keeps me strong when I am faced with a challenging manager or team. It's what allows me to continue to be me, although sometimes a subdued corporate me depending on the environment, and it's what keeps me looking to the future and picking myself up after being rejected. Next time you see me, ask me about the time my proposal for work was rejected by a potential client because my hair and make-up weren't 'corporate' enough. Fellas, I bet you've never had that kind of feedback.

"The way I see it, if you want the rainbow, you gotta put up with the rain." - Dolly Parton

I know that I had to go through the awful times in school and at work. I realize that I had to experience not being valued to see what needs to be challenged and changed. I know that many of you have felt the same way and so you have a choice.

You have a choice to continue to wear the mask and have an easy life of hiding. Or you can join me and become a culture warrior. Working to change the acceptance of bullying and unfair treatment in workplaces and in schools. You can help me transform businesses through helping people transform from corporate lemmings into individuals who feel valued. Everyone should be able to contribute their unique skills, strengths, thoughts and abilities, and be valued for who they are without fear. Perhaps if people are who they truly are we will get better at placing them into roles where they can flourish rather than flounder.

I'm passionate about my mission and until we can change workplaces and corporate environments together we will all continue to experience pain and rejection for being ourselves. But you know what I've discovered? The pain and loss of not being me, is worse.

"It's the mission that matters."
- Buffy the Vampire Slayer

I hope you enjoy this book and you find the lessons and models within it useful for creating a business that delivers results, and that people (including you) love.

Michelle Holland

"Is culture the latest trend in business? No. Business is the latest trend in culture."

Michael Henderson, anthropologist and culture expert

"Culture isn't just how you work or how you feel; it's why you work and feel that way." – Michelle T Holland

Introduction: Culture is the New Black

This is a 'how to' guide. A practical and informative way of taking your business and turning it into one that you love, that others love, and that delivers the results you desire.

Let me be clear. I've never been to war. I'm not a celebrity. I haven't given a TED talk (yet), I haven't been stuck on the top of Mount Everest or lost a limb in a freak accident. I'm just a regular Joe/Jo. Just someone who's worked hard for years figuring out what works and what doesn't. Someone who's helped CEOs and Business Owners to create businesses that they are proud of and delight their customers. This book won't be filled with stories of swashbuckling adventure, or extreme outcomes of success and fame, because they are rare… exciting to read… but rare. What I will give you is real and practical advice has been put together over 20 years of working with businesses of varying sizes to enable them to create the kind of culture they need for their business. I will fill this book with real-world information that real people can use to create a culture that works for their business.

If you are looking for stories of generals, celebrity entrepreneurs or Hollywood stars then you are looking in the wrong book. But if you want real advice that works, is backed up by research, that creates the kind of business that delivers results, and helps you create a place that you and your people will love… then I welcome you because you are in the right place. Stick with me and I will introduce you to a way you can create the business you want.

If there's one thing I know to be true, it's that no matter who you are or how many war stories you have or how much money you make (or don't)… you CAN create or change a business culture.

When I started writing this book, *Culture Inc.* was not the first title that I considered. The original working title was *Culture Is the New Black*. I considered this as a title, because so many people have said to me how 'trendy' culture is right now. "*Everyone's* doing culture…" they tell me.

As someone who's been working in the culture and leadership space for almost 15 years, when I first heard somebody say this, I must admit I got quite offended. With hands on hips and an air of WTF I thought… *"If everyone is 'doing' culture then why are businesses still failing? Why are people still miserable? Why on Monday morning am I faced with a barrage of memes devoted to the 'I HATE MONDAYS' theme?"*

On reflection, my offense evaporated quite quickly and the emotion that replaced it was disbelief and disappointment. Then I started questioning myself.

Is culture a trend? Is culture the new black? Is it just the new management distraction? Is it the new Six Sigma,

Lean or performance management? What is it and why is it that businesses have determined that culture is the new black?

Writer and consultant Michael Henderson, says in his book *Above the Line*, "People often ask me if culture is the new trend in business and my response is, no, business is the new trend in culture." Henderson is an anthropologist and he has studied cultures around the world for years. His comment is brilliant. It resonated strongly with me at the time because I'd already determined that I was going to write this book and share my experiences with creating and transforming business cultures.

Culture is not a trend, it's something that happens regardless of whether we're in business or not in business. There are many different definitions of culture. This causes confusion and because of this there are still a lot of people that are not clear about what culture is, even so called 'culture experts' seem to struggle.

When the term culture is used, its often accompanied by a feeling statement. For example… my culture sucks… or our culture is great. This is not all that helpful. When you dig for more information, the person will say something like "I like my job, but the culture is bad, everyone is unhappy" or "I love my job, everyone is so great to work with."

If this was the only way we defined culture, i.e. whether someone was happy at work or not, then we'd be missing a very large opportunity to create success. Whether someone is happy at work *can* be a result of the culture… but it's not *the* culture.

What is Business Culture?

Let's start by defining business culture so we're all on the same page. I'm asked quite often by executive teams, "Can you simplify culture? Can you make it really easy to understand?", so I often use language like, *"It's how we do things around here."* But it's much more than that. It's the what we do, it's why we do it that way, and it is the baggage we have when we're doing it. It's how we engage in conversations, make decisions, treat each other, make our widgets, and serve our customer.

Culture is not only "How we do things around here", but most importantly, it's WHY we do them that way.

It's how we are expected to work and behave in order to fit in, and specifically it's the support structures that we put into place to reinforce those expectations. Culture is the habits of the people within the business that are consistently reinforced through processes, leadership and rewards.

Like each of us has unconscious behavior (i.e. habits) which guides our behaviors and actions without deliberate thought, we also can have a collective unconscious which we reinforce using systems, processes, practices and language. This is the same in society as it is in business. Remember, business is just a new way of demonstrating our culture.

The Risks of Misunderstanding Culture

Culture is not good or bad. Culture just is. However, if you are not getting the results you want, your people don't love working for you, and your customers are not raving fans it's time to review why.

I'll give you a hint. Your business culture creates these outcomes so if you're not happy with your results, then it's time to create a new culture that delivers the results you want.

Let me take a moment to address the 'bad culture' thinking. When people talk about 'bad' culture they are often talking about things like team conflict, bullying, sexism, exclusion and harassment. This is a challenge for managers who want to create a great workplace environment for their people, however not impossible to change.

I won't focus on this kind of 'culture' because honestly many of these things are illegal and although they still occur, they are not the norm in business any longer. My short advice is address these issues by publicly acknowledging they are happening (note, we are looking for an honest reflection of the behavior without shaming individuals), and then draw a deep line in the sand. Advise all employees that this behavior will *no longer be tolerated* and will be addressed with care through swift and deliberate action. This will take courage and conviction, but it's the only way to truly change it.

If you need inspiration, head to YouTube and watch Chief of Army, Lieutenant-General David Morrison talk about the inappropriate behavior that was evident in the Australian army. He addresses the issues, condemns them publicly, and provides advice on how to deal with infringements against the army's values. It's not enough to give a speech though, you must back it up with action. Deliberate, swift, consistent and appropriate action is what will remove the 'bad' behavior elements from your culture.

> *"The standard that you walk past, is the standard that you accept."* - Lieutenant-General Morrison.

The unfortunate thing about simplifying a complex subject like culture, is that a little bit of knowledge is a dangerous thing. People may develop the misunderstanding that culture change is simple when you simplify it too much. I'm often in a quandary about how I describe culture. My role is to help business leaders truly understand culture and in particular the impact it's having on their business and how to change it. I want to make it simple to engage with them, but in doing so, I worry that this adds to the misconceptions about what it is, and what a business leader needs to do.

I recognize now that my role is not in helping people define culture, but instead help them understand that defining it is only one step along the path of changing culture. There appears to be an intellectual understanding of culture, but not a practical understanding of what creates it, and therefore how to change it.

Too often I witness businesses decide they need to focus on culture, develop a short-term project called 'Culture Change' and give it to the Human Resources (HR) team to manage. I'm going to be blunt here… giving 'culture and leadership transformation' to HR isn't the best method for business transformation. In saying that, let me bring my HR colleagues back to the fold by saying there are extraordinary Human Resources professionals who have learned what it takes to change culture. I'm from a HR background myself so I know it's often where the skill set is nourished. I've had the privilege of working and networking with many brilliant people in this space, however it should not be assumed that all HR professionals have a capability in business transformation.

Your Human Resource Manager may not be the right person to transform your business, but they have an essential role to play. You need the right people, hired, managed, trained and fired to create the culture you need. It's a big part of the puzzle, but it's not the only piece.

If it doesn't fit within Human Resources, where does it sit?

This is a great question and we can debate until the cows come home. Maybe it sits in Human Resources, or it sits in Finance, or it sits in the CEO's office, or it sits with line managers. The reality is, every single person in the organization has a part to play in the development and transformation of a culture. Therefore, it's not that it doesn't fit in HR, it's just it doesn't *only* fit in HR.

Truthfully it doesn't matter what department you allocate the project to, because there's no one department that's going to be broad enough to capture everything there is within the domain of culture. When you are in the process of deliberately 'changing' your culture you may require dedicated internal resources to support you. Ideally, once your culture is established it will become self-sustaining without the need for a dedicated 'culture' resource. Your managers will manage the culture you want, and you can engage an external consultant to do the occasional audit to ensure you are staying on track.

You'll know that your business hasn't embraced culture holistically because every time culture is mentioned people just talk about behaviors or feelings. This is important, but not enough. You'll also hear the term 'engagement' used quite a bit when talking about culture. This is because culture is generally placed firstly and foremost in the people bucket, not the business bucket. Because of that, the focus continues to be about how engaged, satisfied or happy the people are in the business.

Culture is not engagement and engagement is not culture. Engagement may be an outcome of culture but they are not the same thing.

Engagement means the people in the business are satisfied and enjoy working for the business. Because they enjoy working for the business, they'll generally give discretionary effort, recommend the business as a good place to work, and have plans to stay themselves.

The danger with believing that this is your culture, is that you can have a business that's got a highly engaged workforce, because they enjoy the work, or their leader is great, and perhaps they get meaning out of what they do. They may work hard and do a lot more than they need to, but there's no evidence that they are effective. No signs that your customers are reaping the rewards of this happiness. Nothing to say that all that extra effort isn't wasted on running ineffective practices. But hey, if the people are happy at work, that's all that matters… right?

Wrong. One of our Aged Care clients showed high levels of engagement in their engagement survey. It was clear that the people worked their butts off for the business, but would I classify the culture as effective? No way. The discretionary effort was wasted because of the business inefficiencies.

Throughout this book, I'm going to explore the concept of culture as a business function that drives business results. This might upset some people, particularly those that think culture is about making the people in the business happy and satisfied. I'm not going to argue with you if that's what you want... happy and satisfied people. Great, then be nice to them. Give them regular pay raises. Maybe have a pizza night and a reward and recognition program that gives away trips overseas and movie tickets. Have a social club, or free fruit. If you do these things, your people may like your organization. They may like working there and they may even be engaged. However, your customer may not be getting the best results and your business may be failing. This is often the toughest thing for business leaders to grapple with because we all want to be liked. We all want an enjoyable work environment. We all want a place to go where we like the people we work with. As a leader, I like to be liked. This is human behavior. We want and like to be liked. This is not a bad thing; it just doesn't drive business results.

Throughout this book, we're going to talk about customer and business results as the goal for driving the kind of culture you need in a business. The strategies and actions taken as a result of the advice in this book will create a business where your people can be engaged and happy, if that is your goal, in addition to creating great results for your customer and profit in your bottom line – these will be the outcomes of your business culture after fully implementing the advice in this book.

Let's go back to where we started. Defining culture so we are on the same page...

This is the definition I use that underpins the principles of this book:

"Culture is how we do things around here, why we do them that way, and how we feel about what we are doing. Culture is created by the way we form a business and lay the foundation stones that the business is built on... i.e.: the vision, the strategies, the structures, and decision making. Culture is maintained by how the work flows through the business using systems, rewards, policies and processes that continue to reinforce the way we do things and why we do them. And it's demonstrated in the way we feel about the mission of the business, the work we do, the people we work for and with, and our customer.

Therefore, culture is the way the business forms, flows and feels."

Culture is the way the business forms, flows and feels...

Part 1:

Culture Matters

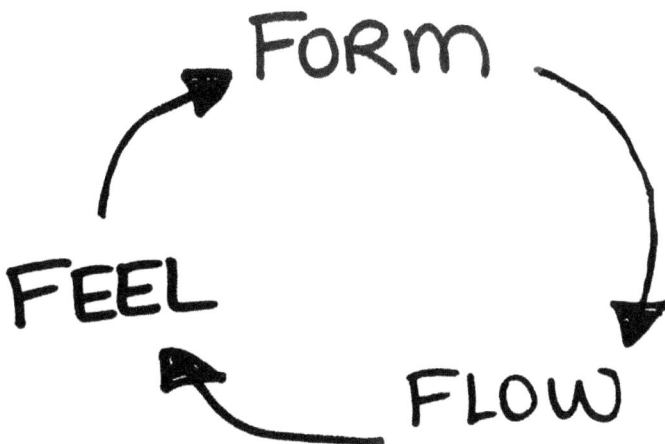

Part 1: Culture Matters

In a 2013 culture and change management survey by Booz & Company, 84% of the 2000 global participants said culture is critically important to business success.

According to McKinsey and Company, 70% of all change initiatives fail.

There's a lot of money and energy being spent on culture and leadership 'programs' thinking they are a magic bullet that will 'fix' the culture.

Training is only one part of a complex puzzle, yet we are using this small jigsaw puzzle piece and trying to understand the whole picture. A half day investment into training, even a two day training program run by a brilliant trainer, won't change your culture. Sorry to be the bearer of bad news because I know that you've spent thousands and thousands on training that hasn't worked.

Training is an important investment for your company to make, but its only one element of change. It's the change management plan, or lack of one should I say, that is the missing link.

Culture transformation can happen quickly if you invest everything you've got into it and take swift deliberate action. Depending on where your culture is now and what you want, expect this to take minimum two to three years of consistent work for real change to occur.

This is why 70% of change programs fail. Most give up and move on to another shiny object after 6–12 months.

You need a real commitment of time and energy if you want real results. From my experience and research what you need for change is:

1. true leadership commitment
2. realistic goals and plans
3. a realistic budget of money and time
4. clear evidence based approach with information and data about current state
5. the courage to take deliberate action and make the changes necessary
6. a change team managing and driving the change, and keeping the businesses optimistic and accountable (one of these people must be the CEO)
7. and most importantly, a real belief that change is possible.

If you are committed there is a way you can change your culture. Following this method and sticking with it will begin to create the culture you need for the success that you want.

I go into this method in Part 2 of this book, but before we go there, let's figure out what is standing in your way from creating this change. If it was as easy as following a step-by-step process then you'd have done it already. The problem is it takes a great deal of courage to acknowledge the things that you and your business are doing that are holding you back from success.

Culture is a complex beast and by understanding the fundamentals more you will be able to engage in the change fully. Stay with me through Part 1, even though I know you are probably an action oriented leader and you want to jump to the solution in Part 2, but isn't that what you always do?

If you do the same thing you've always done, then you will get the same thing you've always got… thanks Marshall Goldsmith, Coaching Guru, for that piece of wisdom.

Over the next few chapters I will introduce you to the potential pitfalls and dangers that you may need to address to set yourself up for a successful outcome, and provide you with information, case studies and evidence that builds a case for culture transformation. You'll recognize that there is only one choice to make.

Transform.

Chapter 1:
Culture Happens

"Change is the only constant, whether it's in music, culture, dance or fashion."

Sonu Nigam, musician

> *"Creating a high performing culture can be as simple as 'don't be a jerk, and get shit done.' Crude yet effective."* – Michelle T Holland

Chapter 1: Culture Happens

If you don't do culture, culture will do you. This is something that I've said many times throughout my career. Generally, I'm responding to a comment like, "*I don't have time to* do *culture.*"

The thing is… culture is not something that you *do*, culture just *is*. Culture happens when you're not looking. Culture happens when you're working hard to deliver outcomes for your client. Culture happens when you're having a conversation in the lunch room. Culture just happens.

"Culture is the way the business forms, flows and feels."

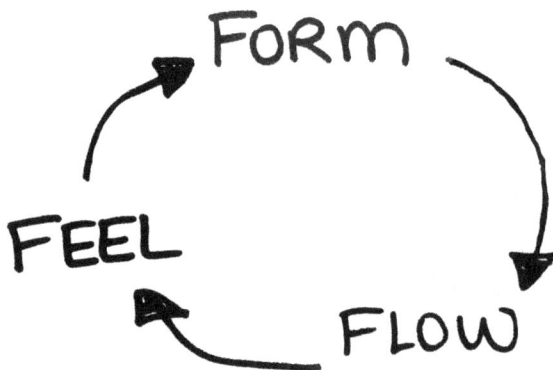

FORM

FEEL

FLOW

"I don't have time to do culture" is a comment said by at least one manager, often more, when I'm speaking with a group of managers who are about to embark on a culture change program. Usually their CEO, or their Head of Human Resources, has asked me to come in because they have identified that there are elements of the business that are holding them back. The room is full of very busy managers who have been asked to turn up and have been told that they are responsible for the culture 'problems', so they need to learn how to fix them.

Not surprising the very busy manager responds to this narrow-minded criticism with an apathetic attendance at a 'culture workshop'. I never judge a person for this comment because culture change is more complex than just telling a manager to 'fix the problems'. I don't judge, but I do educate them about the dangers of saying it.

Culture change takes effort and know-how. If you want to change your culture because of the problems that you are seeing, then you need to have the right approach and the right people helping you do it. The approach my team and I use is based in the FORM, FLOW and FEEL model.

In the Introduction, I defined culture as the form, flow and feel of a business. Let me briefly introduce you to the model.

FORM

When you set up, or FORM, a new business you consider the vision, the mission, the strategy, the product, the service delivery model, the sales model and the people who will manage these things. If you have the luxury to form your brand and culture from scratch then you are in a fortunate position, and well done for grabbing this book early in your journey, if you implement the principles from this book you will have a greater chance of long term sustainable, and satisfying success.

Most businesses I work with are well established and have often become overwhelmed by the outcomes of their culture. That is the FEEL part of the model. This is the wrong focus when it comes to culture. When you only focus on the FEEL you won't change your culture.

We'll examine this further in Chapter 7, but essentially the FORM aspects of the business that need to be addressed first are:

- The vision
- The mission
- The values
- The strategy
- The structures*
- The customer expectation
- The leadership expectation

*Structures consist of things like workforce/team structures, and management decision making structures, financial structures, governance, and infrastructure.

FLOW

Understanding how expectations and work flows through the business is important to understanding how people in the business come to 'understand' how they must work and behave in order for them to fit into the current culture.

FLOW will be examined in detail in Chapter 8, but simply it is:

- The processes, policies, and practices
- The management systems*
- The reward systems

- The leadership capability and actions
- The communication
- The behavior, technical capabilities and actions

*Management systems includes how decisions are made, how people are selected, how work is planned, and how performance is measured and rewarded.

When we focus on FLOW we are speaking of the formal systems of work that provide a framework for the work of the business.

Later in the book we'll talk practically about creating a plan for transformation, this will give you an organized method to create change in your business. However, if you know that your business would respond better to a strict system then have a look at the Australian Business Excellence Framework, or Six Sigma, or Lean. When implemented properly they are excellent. When implemented poorly they cause more problems to the culture than they are worth. Choose carefully, and implement even more carefully.

FEEL

A result of the culture and the reinforcing systems determines how we **feel** about the business. This is the part of the culture that gets the most airtime in business. The reason being that we are very emotional creatures and therefore if something doesn't feel good we talk about it.

FEEL in this model falls in the following general categories:

- Relationships
- Motivation
- Enjoyment/satisfaction

- Customer loyalty
- Results
- Agility

Each of these areas are influenced by the culture and are also influenced by other things outside of the business. For example, a relationship can dissolve due to personal reasons or conflict even if the culture is strong, engagement can be high because the person loves their profession at the same time as hating their business, satisfaction can change with the introduction of a new manager or team mate, and of course a self-actualized person will be motivated despite the culture.

When I work with organizations they have a tendency to want to tackle this stuff first, and many times it's the only thing that they discuss or apply funding to. Therefore, they allocate great funds to training programs and nothing else. They don't focus on the expectations and flow of work, and rarely do they think to address the FORM elements that are the foundations of the business. There is no surprise that most culture change programs fail when this is the approach. There must be an integrated approach to change or failure is inevitable.

Unfortunately, because of the fickle nature of feelings, by targeting these things only, you can achieve a quick boost to the FEEL of the business and therefore the manager thinks it's 'fixed'. However, it requires a more thorough investigation and plan to create a sustainable change. Don't despair if you have spent lots of money on training, all is not lost.

If you have a headache every morning for a month and all you do is take a painkiller you can be masking a bigger problem that won't be fixed via a tablet. However sometimes you need to take the tablet so the brain fog lifts so you can come up with a better solution. Your spending or me it's what their manager 'tells' them to do. This is true for the formal expectations. However, when I explore further they begin to tell me about the day-to-day ways that expectations are truly understood by the people. Expectations start from formal conversations and planning to just watching people around the business. Observing what they do and how they get rewarded is often a stronger determinant of the *real* expectations of the business. Let's pause and talk about rewards for a moment because they are critical to the culture story.

When I say rewards in the context of work, what may spring to mind is salary, holidays, staff awards, appreciation programs, employee of the month, gift certificates, tickets to the movies, or a trip the Bahamas.

29

These are formal mechanisms of rewarding for performance at work. They may be governed and they even may be successful in causing satisfaction and engagement. However, there is a better reward that often gets overlooked.

What we overlook is how our brain gets a 'reward' signal for the simplest of things. The greatest reward of all is the release of serotonin.

Serotonin, is the hormone that is released when we experience pleasure. The purpose of serotonin is to reinforce activities that are pleasurable to our brain and bodies. The more times serotonin is released for a behavior, the more we know what behavior to repeat. Serotonin can be quite addictive which is great when we feel rewarded for eating a salad or going for a walk. The annoying part is that serotonin doesn't differentiate between helpful behavior and unhelpful behavior.

We may experience a burst of serotonin from a simple pat on the back when another person thinks we've done something well. This burst tells us that we are on the right track, even if that track is eating chocolate, stealing cars or managing a useless process over and over at work. This burst is heightened when it comes from a person we respect or believe is our superior. For example, if our older brother who is our hero gives us a 'pat on the back' for stealing cars, our serotonin is released. If he does this often enough, and we're not self-actualized, then it will likely be the behavior that we seek to repeat.

Imagine this scenario – you have a manager and this manager is very passionate about the work that they do. They are very driven and want to get big results from their team. They have provided a very clear business plan of all the elements that their team need to complete to enable them to reach the goal that they have set. They are a nice person, but you also know that they are not pleased with people who question their business plan.

You have seen it before. You've seen people get shut down or get ignored in meetings when they question the plan, and of course you don't want that. You look at that business plan and you see an element that's not going to work. It's not going to deliver the results that the leader is looking for, in fact it may stand in the way of delivering the results that this leader and team want to get. What do you do?

Well, if you want that nice burst of serotonin, you'll do the thing that's going to get you the pat on the back. You know that if you question this manager, he may shut you down or tell you that your idea is not worth listening to. You know that if you ask a question, it will delay the outcome and the team won't be pleased with you.

These are the clues to the 'right' behavior that you see at work. You know logically that the best course of action for the business is to question, but the best outcome for you personally is to take no action. This is the safe course of action. The course that will protect you from the harm you have observed happening to others.

When you make the decision to avoid the pain, you get a release of serotonin. Your brain gives you a congratulations for not taking action! This is happening in every single person, in every single organization, everywhere.

One of our basic human instincts is to reduce pain and seek pleasure…

To create change personally we must find ways to fight our biological instinct and experience the pain. If we are serotonin addicts – which many of us are – it's even harder. Is it any wonder that our businesses aren't functioning how we want them to? Who wants to change something and feel pain, when they could leave it the same and feel pleasure?

This is why it's essential to have structure, know-how and a plan for change, because if we left it to chance… status quo will reign supreme!

Culture Happens Around Us and to Us

Culture is happening around us all the time. We're affected by the environment that we're working in, we're affected by the people around us, we're affected by the customers and their expectations. Usually when a culture struggle happens it is when expectations change. Whether it's your expectations, or the expectations of someone else. When the expectations change that's when the struggle begins. Usually expectations change over a period of time and you might not notice them changing. However, everyone's experienced a new CEO or a new boss coming in and wanting to make an immediate change.

It's great to make swift decisions and immediate change, when it's needed, just be aware the culture you are trying to change is the culture that you are working in. You need to fight against the culture tide to make change. This is challenging because the culture will fight against you.

It's like a bungee cord that's attached to your waistband. You can run along, achieving things, moving in a direction that you want to go, and then all of a sudden the slack in the bungee cord stops, and it becomes really difficult to move forward, you may struggle and keep pulling against it, but at some point, it gets too much for you and *PING* you are pulled backwards. Culture holds on tight and is rarely gentle when it pulls you back in.

This ping is the reason that so many managers and staff tell me they don't have the time to 'do' culture. They are actually talking about the effort and energy it takes to create change. Not only are they having to change on a collective basis, but usually they are also engaged in a personal struggle with change.

The evidence is clear that if you want a business that delivers results and people love, you have got to do culture. In the next couple of chapters, we'll talk about the business case for a great culture and what happens when you don't focus on it.

Key Take-away

It's essential to have structure, know-how and a plan for change, because if we left it to chance… status quo will reign supreme!

Self-coaching Questions

- How am I contributing to the culture right now?
- What behavior and actions am I engaging in that holds our culture exactly where it is?

With the right culture you get...

CUSTOMER RESULTS

45%
Higher Customer
Loyalty

55%
Higher Customer
Satisfaction

32%
Better Customer
Outcomes

EMPLOYEE RESULTS

36%
Higher Employee
Motivation

18%
More Likely
to Stay

26%
More Satisfied
at Work

TEAM RESULTS

28%
Better Team
Work

30%
Better at
Collaboration

20%
Increase in Team
Productivity

BUSINESS RESULTS

20%
Increased
Productivity

32%
Increased
Quality

54%
Greater Market
Adability

Note: Statistics from the book: "Why culture and leadership matter". Research and development by Robert A Cooke Phd, and J Clayton Lafferty Phd, Human Synergistics International.

Chapter 2:
Your Culture IS your Brand

"What's the best way to build a brand for the long term? In a word: culture."

Tony Hsieh, CEO, Zappos

> *"Culture isn't something you do, it just is. The question remains, is it the culture you need to deliver the outcomes your customers have been promised?"* – Michelle T Holland

Chapter 2: Your Culture IS your Brand

Just imagine that you work in an organization, or own a business, that delivers results exactly how you want it to. Not just delivers the 3result that you want, but also delivers them in a way which makes you proud and energized, ensures your people love coming to work and has your customers lining up at your door.

Just take a moment and imagine that business…. sigh… sounds good doesn't it?

Think about your current reality. Does it fulfill that dream? Are you fulfilled by what you are experiencing? Does everyone love coming to work? Do your customers love interacting with your business?

I'm using that word *love* quite deliberately. Success doesn't happen by accident, it happens through deliberate action. When I think about my own success I define it as a balance of financial, spiritual (i.e. purpose/meaning) and humanistic experiences that fill me with joy. Success is something that you must define yourself but for argument's sake we'll define success here as having a business which is a joy to work for, is profitable, has a meaningful impact on the world, and whose customers advocate for it, broadly and loudly. Success like this doesn't show up in a business that people just *like*. And it definitely doesn't happen in a business where people go because there isn't an alternative.

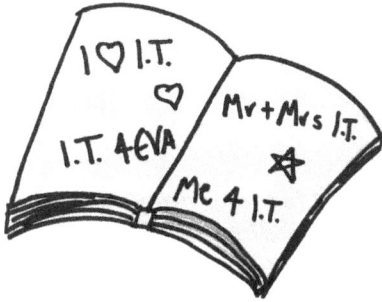

Consider a business that you return to time and time again. It may be your local coffee shop, or bookshop, or hairdresser. I know a lot of you are leaders, business founders and CEOs reading this book, so I bet that you drink a lot of coffee (or wine… depending on the stage of your journey) but let's talk coffee. If you drink coffee, you have a favorite coffee shop. This is a coffee shop that you go into regularly. You can get a good cup of coffee in other places, but this one keeps drawing you back. When you think about it closely, I'm willing to make a bet that it's the environment and the people that are drawing you back… in addition to your addiction to that delicious black goodness.

A dear friend of mine, Mike, was talking to me about a coffee shop that he quite regularly goes into. He explained that the coffee is okay, it's not brilliant or perfect by any means and he knows there are much better coffee shops that produce better coffee. But he keeps going back. He admitted that it was the customer service officer behind the counter that kept him drinking coffee there. He told me, with visible joy, that she was always friendly, she remembers his coffee order, she says "Good morning" and " How was your day?" and she treats him as an individual. Simple, yet effective because the interaction with her made him feel great. As a customer, it made him want to go back to that coffee shop, not because they deliver the best product, but because of the way they made him feel.

Marketing research and human behaviorists tell us that we make emotional decisions more often than logical ones. It seems illogical, but the way a business makes us feel is more important to our buying decision than price or quality. Neuroscientist Antonio Damasio even argues that emotional decisions are better than logical ones. Given this research and the research of others that supports this claim, why aren't more businesses working on the heart of their business… the culture and how it makes the customer feel?

> *"I've learned that people will forget what you said, people will forget what you did, but people will never forget how you made them feel."*
> – Maya Angelou

Think about the effect your people have on your customer/sales/repeat business, and now think about how your culture impacts your people. Is your culture one that encourages fun, caring and energy, or are your people experiencing a negative uninspiring environment? The culture that your people experience is the outcome that your customer will receive.

Like that coffee shop, the focus must be on making the customer experience unforgettable. Don't think that having a great service experience gives you license to deliver a substandard product, it doesn't. Like I said, he told me the coffee is good there, it's not best coffee – but it's good and the service is excellent, which makes him go back. If the coffee was terrible, he'd find somewhere else.

It's important to note that if your product is amazing and your service is only good (or bad), it won't make your customers love you. However, if your product is good, and your customer experience is exceptional you will be forgiven for product teething problems.

Simon Sinek's book *Start With Why* discusses the emotional connection people have to companies. He explains how Apple clearly articulate their *why*, their purpose, the meaning of their brand and he argues that this is the reason people love Apple and forgive them when their product has problems.

However, it's only one part of the puzzle. The people who work for Apple believe in Apple's *why* and are skilled in living the Apple values. Apple is focused on the user experience even more than the technical aspects of their products. Therefore, the people who work at Apple, and in Apple stores, work hard to produce an experience and a product that delights their customers.

Apple wouldn't have become the Apple it is today, if it wasn't for the people who were working there. If it wasn't for the culture that has been established at Apple. If they weren't clear about their mission it would be difficult for people to get behind them and follow them into the unknown. Apple would never be the Apple that it is today without the focus they have on the type of brand, culture, and customer experience that they wanted to create.

I'm not going to tell you that Apple has the perfect culture – it doesn't. In fact, Steve Jobs was criticized for his leadership style throughout his career. The story of Jobs is fascinating, particularly when you look at the leader's role in culture which we will explore later in this book. Notwithstanding the impact of an individual leader, as a company they are damn good at making sure their people love Apple and therefore so do their customers.

Zappos is another great example of where culture is the driver of their brand. Tony Hsieh, the CEO of Zappos, in his book *Delivering Happiness* talks extensively about the focus and attention that he put into building the Zappos' business culture. Hsieh's message is clear that Zappos is a purpose-led business and he's clear that their culture is the secret to why their customers love them and keep coming back. Hsieh talks about it from an internal people culture point of view and

Sinek talks about it from a marketing point of view. When you read both books you notice that actually… it's the same message. The way your company communicates internally and externally will drive your success and your sales.

The simple message is, your culture is your brand, and your culture will determine how people talk about you – whether you have set it up deliberately or not. The way in which your customer interacts with your business is a direct result of the culture that you have. If you have people working within your business who don't care about your business, they don't like the manager that they're working for, and they think the process and the practices are not helpful, your customer is never going to get the best experience.

Your customer may still get an outcome, but if you're not focused on the way in which you're delivering that service or product, then I would question if they are getting the best outcome you could deliver them.

If you're not giving your customer an amazing experience, someone else will.

This is why I use the word *love,* because love isn't something that we can take for granted. Love is something that we have to actively participate in. The culture of your business is something you actively participate in. The culture of your business right now is representing who you are to your customer.

When you are honest with yourself, truly honest, when you're having a 'middle of the night' conversation with yourself and nobody else is looking… is your business delivering the kind of results that you dreamed of when you started?

Think back to when you first started that business, or when you first joined your organization, think about the vision that you had. Think about what you wanted to achieve, and tell me – is your business living up your expectations? Because if it's not then it's certainly not living up to your customers' expectations.

We live in a high-tech world and I truly believe that customer interaction and customers' experience is actually the thing that sets one business apart from another. In a high-tech world, high touch is essential if you want to stand out from the crowd.

Remember what Damasio says about emotional decision making? In essence he is saying that people want to interact with people. What marketers have always known is we'll buy more when we feel valued. This is why all the commercials on TV have a lovely happy smiling person talking about the 'thing' they want you to buy. If it was just about the washing powder then they should show the powder, and the results of using the powder. There is no need to have a human in the commercial… except that we want to connect with a person. We need to emotionally connect to buy that powder, and I don't know about you, but washing powder doesn't pluck my emotion strings but a puppy or a baby all snuggly in a fluffy blanket… I'm sold. We want the convenience of technology, AND we want to interact with people. When you remove the human interaction completely from a business, it loses its heart and it loses its soul.

A number of years ago, I remember watching the big four Australian banks, Westpac, ANZ, the Commonwealth Bank and the National Australian Bank, go through a transition process with their customer service. I watched this intimately because my mum worked for a bank at the time. The changes that they went through were focused on creating greater efficiencies for the business, and their customers, utilizing technology to improve service delivery.

Brilliant goal, but the mistake the banks made was instead of using technology to add to the customer experience, they thought that customers wanted technology to replace people in the customer experience. They quickly found out that by replacing their people and bank tellers with automatic machines, they lost their edge in customer service. By making key services online or offshore, they lost their ability to connect to the customer. Small banks and credit unions that connected with the community began to rise in popularity.

Recently these same banks are transitioning again to improve the customer experience. A local branch that I go into has created a customer experience that is mimicking a doctor's office. There are technology options in the branch, including a suite of automatic banking machines to utilize. However, the placement of these machines is off to the side of an open space which has lounge chairs. It's a very inviting space and considering it's a bank, it's an unusual space to feel that you are invited into. But it has that feeling of waiting for someone to help you and serve you. When you're using the technology, there's always someone in the bank ready to help you if you need help. There's a friendly face standing behind the counter to greet you.

Gone are the days when there were ten bank tellers standing behind the desk waiting to serve you. But also gone are the days where you were told to do everything online. We're encouraged to use the automated machines of course, but their clever messaging doesn't feel like it's the only alternative anymore. We have these inviting, comfortable spaces with people who are going to help us.

So why am I talking about marketing and the customer experience in a book about culture?

Because the culture you have now is the experience you are giving your customer. If we remember our definition of culture, it's 'the way the business forms, flows and feels', and the outcome of these things influence the customer's decision to buy... or not.

The banks learned a very serious lesson in what their customers expected from them. Although their profit margins may have increased, their reputation declined and their customers began to question their motives. They discovered it wasn't about a quick banking experience, because I can get that anywhere. It wasn't a cheap interest rate, because they can negotiate that anywhere.

It was feeling that they were being cared for, that they were being looked after, that they were being welcomed into the business. They want to develop a relationship with the bank because at the heart of an interaction with a bank is emotion. Money can build huge amounts of fear, anxiety, excitement and confusion in the average person. Having a company that you trust to look after your money and therefore look after you and your family is a big draw card for staying with a bank. As soon as trust is established, or broken, between a customer and their bank a 'stay or go' decision is imminent. The banks know this and they are transitioning back to more high touch environment to complement their high tech.

Your culture is your brand, whether you want to believe it or not.

Key Take-away

When your people are having a terrible experience with your business, then your customers will also... and vice versa.

Self-coaching Questions

- How can I ensure my customers are getting the best experience from my business?
- What is the best decision/action for the organization, to meet its purpose?

Chapter 3:
When Good Cultures go Bad

> *"It is our choices... that show what we truly are, far more than our abilities."*
>
> JK Rowling, author

"If you don't manage your culture, your culture will manage you." – Michelle T Holland

Chapter 3: When Good Cultures go Bad

We can blame all sorts of things for the culture we have. The excuses I regularly hear are not completely without merit, but if change and business effectiveness is the end-game, what is to be gained from making excuses… even if they appear real.

Excuses are fundamentally a fear of blame. The business leader doesn't want to be blamed. The people leader doesn't want to be blamed. The CEO doesn't want to be blamed. So, they blame 'the business' – the business does this, the business does that, the business does whatever. Think about that for a moment… what the hell is 'the business' anyway? The business is a complete nebulous concept and really, other than registering a company name and number, the business is the form, flow and feel of the work activities that people do… i.e. the culture. It is the people, it is the structures, it is the things that we put in place to make it so. It's you.

I'm going to tell you about five excuses that I hear on a regular basis. I've chosen these five because they are the main ones that I hear from business leaders and employees on why their culture is the way it is or why they cannot change it to be anything else. You may or may have not said one of these things before. I'm not putting this here to shame anyone. No judgement, just observations.

The reason I want to talk to you about excuses is because these are the things that are getting in your way of changing the culture properly. If you have heard yourself say these things, please be aware that you are holding yourself back from something great.

Excuse # 1: We have no time and no money for culture change.

If I had a dollar for every time I have heard this I could pay for a culture change program for every business in Australia. I believe the reason that they're using this excuse is because they quite legitimately believe that it takes a lot of time and a lot of money to change their culture.

Traditionally businesses have not fully understood what it takes to shift their culture and therefore they'll assume that they know. They go to a consultant or a training organization who sells a very high-end, expensive training program for their staff or a leadership program for their leaders. They pay for this very expensive program sometimes upwards of a million dollars in training for their leaders and don't get the culture change results that they were hoping for.

It's not to say that good things don't come out of training programs, they do. I'm a consultant too and know that providing a robust training program is a benefit for the business. It helps engage staff and starts a different kind of conversation at work. It's the spending of a million dollars on a training program without anything else supporting the change program that I have a problem with.

Look, let's get real, sales people have one outcome in mind… sales of their training program. They aren't all that concerned about the long-term effect. They focus on the short-term effect, the feel of the program. I don't want to upset all of the trainers out there because many of the programs are excellent and have a valuable impact on many individuals. But because they generally aren't part of a fully integrated culture transformation program they won't have a culture transformation effect.

It takes time and money for culture to change, but not as much as you think.

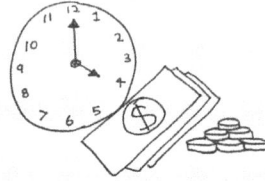

I understand where the 'I don't have money for culture change' comes from. I'm here to tell you that if you invest wisely, it doesn't take millions of dollars to shift your culture.

The 'no time for culture' however is a real catch-22. It is true that you need to put time and effort into shifting culture. Most business leaders are too busy working hard to maintain the current culture to create the kind of change that is needed to shift the culture. They are on the hamster wheel and find it hard to get off so they can change the processes that are causing them so much work and pain.

Because of the way we structure businesses and put systems in place, it means that we must unpick all those structural systems that we put into place before we can create the kind of culture that we want to create. Sounds exhausting, right? Well it is when you don't focus on the right things. Do the first things first, as Stephen Covey would say.

There is time investment in changing the culture. I think it's more time than money that's needed but we tend to get wrapped up in the money. When you have a systematic way of being able to tackle these issues, then the time and money is invested wisely.

The excuse of "*I haven't got the time or money for culture change*" is a direct result of the problematic and ineffectual culture change activities that have been sold to you in the past.

In part two of this book I go through a systematic way of being able to develop a culture change program for yourself. One that shows you where you should put your time and your money so this is no longer an excuse.

Excuse # 2: Culture is something HR does.

Sigh.... every time I hear somebody say "Culture is HR's job" or "I don't have time to work on the HR stuff" or "Managers need more soft skills" it makes me cringe and sigh a long frustrated sigh. Whether it comes from leaders and employees in the business or comes from HR staff – let me tell you it comes from both – it's a cop-out.

When I hear somebody talking this way I know straight away that they do not understand what culture is. This excuse is essentially saying "I've got a practical job to do – I need to move that box from point A to point B – and anything that gets in my way to be able to do that is not valued by me." The 'HR stuff' term usually surfaces when we start talking about managing staff, people systems, communication, leadership and behavior change.

The excuse-maker is generally a person who values quick outcomes and working alone. Unfortunately many team leaders have this as their natural default. Over time businesses have changed hiring practices, but in the 70s and 80s the main way you moved into a position of authority was due to the length of time you spent in your technical role. Longest tenure became the catalyst for leadership promotion. Thankfully that practice has changed and many leaders are selected based on their ability to manage a team. However, many of the people selected in the 70s and 80s are still in business, or at least their attitudes remain in business because they have been passed onto the next generation through mentoring, role-modelling and training.

Great business leaders recognize that communication, managing people, being compassionate, and holding people accountable for their behavior *is* their job. If the leader is focused on moving the box from point A to point B then they're actually not a leader, they're a worker. The distinction is that you have a title of leader or manager and you have been given a privileged position. You have been given a position whereby you are responsible for the performance of others and your performance should be measured on that, not your ability to move the box.

Let's be frank, culture and leadership are not a 'HR thing', it's much broader as I hope you are coming to recognize. If businesses are not willing to look beyond HR when talking about culture then they are never going to get the result they need. Culture determines how that box is being moved, and sometimes if it's moved at all. It prescribes what the customer is receiving as a result of moving that box from A to B.

Culture is the fundamental aspect of whether or not the customer gets the best results or they just get a result – does that sound like HR's job?

Excuse # 3: People are here to work.

People are here to work, often followed up with '*not to have fun*'. Isn't it sad to think you can't both work and have fun. If you believe that you can either work or you can have fun, then you are missing out on having a long happy life. This comment is often said by someone with a very sour face who clearly doesn't understand how much research has been conducted on the value of fun at work. We spend a great deal of time at work, so why shouldn't it also be enjoyable?

In his book *Play*, author and psychiatrist Stuart Brown, MD, who is also the founder of the National Institute for Play, states, "When employees have the opportunity to play, they actually increase their productivity, engagement and morale." Dr Brown goes on to say, "Not only does having a playful atmosphere attract young talent, but experts say play at work can boost creativity and productivity in people of all ages. There is good evidence that if you allow employees to engage in something they want to do which is playful, there are better outcomes in terms of productivity and motivation."

The comment also assumes that culture is frivolous. People are here to work. I must admit I hear this a lot particularly in manufacturing-style businesses or businesses where there is a lot of task emphasis in the role. For example, I've worked with organizations where there are many people who are working on fixing roads, maintaining parks, taking the rubbish away, maintaining the cleanliness and the operation of the city. These roles tend to be very task-oriented and often thankless. They have a long list of activities that they need to achieve by the time they finish their shift. The danger with this kind of role is that it becomes all about task, it becomes all about the check in the box on the work order form, or the customer relationship management system. It's all about checking it off.

To have an effective business and have a great culture that delivers the outcomes that you want for your customer in the most effective, efficient and innovative way, you must have people demonstrating an ability and desire to create change and improve systems. It must be a focus of your program and be the norm in people's behavior.

Businesses that understand that attitude and behavior is 50% of the person's performance, and they reward and manage this way, have much stronger cultures. I speak to managers so often who say, "I have an employee that does their job really well, but their attitude and behavior is terrible." My response is always, well if their behavior is that bad then they aren't doing their job well at all (and in my head, I'm thinking… 'and neither are you by allowing them to behave that way').

The work will happen regardless, however the choice is in 'how' that work happens. Therefore why wouldn't you choose a 'how' that is more enjoyable and more effective, rather than the same old, same old?

People are here to work, absolutely they are. Actually they are here to serve the customer. Your customer deserves the best possible result and the best possible service, and they receive that when people in your business think about the way in which they are delivering results… not just the task that they are doing.

Excuse # 4: But the people in our business "are empowered."

If you didn't notice I wrote that one with a slight sarcastic inflection. A business leader tells me that their people can make change. They show me the written values or innovation/change policy. Unfortunately, what they fail to show me is that their systems support the application of these values and polices.

When investigating empowerment I look for evidence that shows how an employee can make a change in a business.

To make a practical change, small or large, in a business you need several elements:

- Information, evidence and data to explore the change;
- Capability of the project team members to develop and deploy the change;
- The resources, budget, tools, systems – or the ability to get them; and
- Decision making authority.

And when I hear people say, "our employees are empowered," I look for evidence of the above dot points before looking at attitudes. The evidence of empowerment will be seen in the outcomes. There will be a system in place, not a just a policy, which facilitates change. The employees can make a change without going through levels and levels... and levels of management. The evidence of empowerment is in the structures that help a person make a decision on their own. They know the boundaries in which they can make those decisions. When people are empowered through systems, you have an effective culture.

When the above elements are not available to the employee, or they are too hard to come by, change can still happen. The change will happen through the courage, desire and sheer tenacity of the individual employee. The problem with seeing this as the definition of empowerment means that the support structures that get in the way will never change and the employee who is making change becomes worn out, or burnt out, or singled out, and will leave. It's exhausting to work in a business where the resistance to change is reinforced in the business systems.

Yes, empowerment can be an innate ability within people. I know that I've never waited for permission to make a change and when I didn't have the authority or the resources to make the change I wanted, I went and found them. I made change, but there were times throughout my career where I didn't feel empowered to make change and it came with a personal cost. A General Manager at a business I worked in years ago said to me, "People create great things in this organization despite the culture, not because of it." He was not a lone wolf in experiencing that.

Every human being has the ability to have a new idea. A business can't make someone come up with a new idea and nor can they stop them from coming up with a new idea. However, a business or management structure can sure as heck stop that idea coming to fruition.

Empowerment is supported by a structural process. If you think that your people are empowered and yet you're still not getting the results that you want to get, start looking at the decision-making systems, the performance systems, and customer service systems that you have in place to see how easy it is for a front line employee to make a decision or take action to change the outcome for a customer. Look at the reward and punishment structures that may be standing in the way. Don't forget – budget is a structure.

Excuse # 5. But we're already successful so our culture works.

I love this one. My inner monologue goes… why have you called me to talk with you about culture then… but my question to them is, "So what is success for you?"

Most of the time they start with success being the outcomes that they provide for their customers, which is a good place to start. They tell me about their profit or their financial turnover, or that their business has been around for 60 years. You can have a business that stays around for 60 years and doesn't have an effective culture. They may just have a niche market, maybe a monopoly. You find this a lot within government organizations.
Government organizations tend to have a monopoly. They are responsible for a specific element whereby they don't have any competition (or limited). So therefore, they are around for a long period. They have money to spend because their customers have to pay taxes, and they have a limited choice to go elsewhere.

In Australia several years ago, Telstra, or Telecom as it was called back then, was a government-owned telecommunications company. They were a cumbersome, big organization and held the monopoly to provide phone services to the Australian people. They started as Telecom in the 70s, and were privatized in the 90s.

They received payments from their customers and stayed in business but they did not appear to have an effective culture. As soon as the regulations changed to create an open market, their customers flooded away from them, losing huge amounts of market share. When they were first privatized the share price was upwards of $7, and now (at the time of printing) their share price is around $3.50. This of course is only one outcome of success, but as an indicator of their culture... it's a good one.

Even today, 20 years on, Telstra is still around. It is now a commercial entity that has to fight for its customers the same as other telecom providers do. They continue to hold the majority share of the market at 41% in 2017. However, to go from 100% only 25 years ago to losing 60% of their customer base because their customers were offered a choice had to be a blow.

When you ask people why they are with Telstra, they don't commonly say it's because of their great service. They don't often say it's because they are easy to work with. In fact, generally they say, "Well it's because they own the infrastructure so I might as well be with them." I'm not saying Telstra hasn't done some great work, they have, and they continue to do good work. However, when you review the evidence across the last 25 years of their history it appears that they struggled after being a government-owned organization and a monopoly to transform into a commercial entity. A colleague of mine worked at Telstra for a number of years during the early stages and they told me that Telstra struggled at first to create a culture that supported the new market pressure. I tell you this not to discredit Telstra, in fact I am a customer and have recently experienced an increase in customer experience, I tell you this story to show you the power of change and the power of having the right kind of culture to support the change.

Get rid of the excuses.

If you are not getting the results you want, and you want to change that, then you must stop the denial, the avoidance and the opposition and just get on with the job of changing the culture. As with any change, it can happen simply if you get out of your own way.

Currently you and your business is working very hard to keep the culture exactly the way it is through all the activities that you are engaged in and the conversations that you are having with each other. If the excuses resonate, then you and your people are avoiding the work required to change your culture and until you acknowledge that, it won't change.

Let's have a look at a couple of other things that are getting in the way of your success and then we'll get into the process of changing them.

Key Take-away

Notwithstanding the fact that we are all human and a transition from one culture to another is a hard journey, we need to be aware of the excuses that we are using to avoid doing the work that is needed.

Self-coaching Questions

- How are you using excuses to avoid change?
- What reasons have you (or your colleagues) created so you won't look at your culture deeply?
- Are you afraid to ask the question because you don't want to hear the answer?

Chapter 4:
Leading Transformation

> *"The role of a creative leader is not to have all the ideas; it's to create a culture where everyone can have ideas and feel that they're valued."*

Ken Robinson, Creativity and Education Thought Leader

"Great leaders create great businesses – why are people still surprised by this?" – Michelle T Holland

Chapter 4: Leading Transformation

About two years before this book was written, a coaching client sat with me and shared her culture experiences from the past. She had worked in a professional services firm where the culture was toxic. She resigned because of the damage it was doing to her wellbeing. After trying another organization, she left quickly because of the same kind of culture. She was frustrated and so she established her own business. Our coaching agenda focused on helping her establish an effective and high performing culture from day one. As we were talking she reflected on the previous business she had worked for and said, "I don't want my culture to be that toxic. I'm worried that I won't be a good leader and I know that the fish rots from the head."

Fast forward six months to another client, in another business, and they were telling me about the culture they were in and they wanted the CEO to make some changes. "The CEO needs to change his ways, because the fish rots from the head."

About two months before finishing this book I was presenting a culture development workshop and a participant looked at me and quite seriously said, "Well, there's nothing I can do about the culture because the fish rots from the head."

Is your fish rotting?

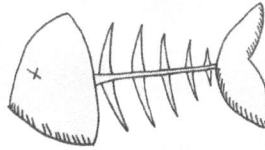

At this point I decided that I had heard this saying too many times. Early on in my career, I would think "Yes – absolutely you're right." Until I became a business leader myself and when I heard it again, it distressed and upset me. It had this effect on me because of how often I worked with great business leaders, executives, and CEOs, who recognize the obligations, the privilege, and the loneliness of the leader. After years of working with these leaders who admitted to their struggle, and others who did not, I was convinced that the role of the leader in culture is quintessential in success.

The phrase "the fish rots from the head" is a dreadful thing to say, and comes from the understanding that leadership is the cause of culture. There is quite a bit of research that shows that the culture of the business is influenced strongly by the leadership. There's a saying that many change agents use which is '75% of the culture is influenced by the leadership'. I've looked for the actual research study that proposed this and have been yet to find it. However, the countless studies and research I have found shows that the quality of leadership and the style of the leaders is directly correlated to the culture outcomes and employee satisfaction.

For example, a study conducted by International Management Institute of New Dehli (Popli and Rizvi 2017) shows a direct link between the leadership style and the employee's engagement levels. It's not a new discovery either – in 1962 Fleishman and Harris determined a direct link between the leader and 'subordinate' relationship, and the outcomes it produced. The study showed that an increased relationship between these parties produced higher outcomes in performance, engagement and satisfaction. So whether it's 75% or not, leadership has a significant impact on the culture.

In my experience working with businesses, you can quite clearly see that the style of the leader is similar to, or at minimum influences the culture of the team or business. In my consulting practice, I utilize profiling tools that enable me to analyze the style of the leader and compare it to the culture of the business. Regularly, the leader's style is very similar to the culture, but not always.

"The fish rots from the head" is an unfair assessment when thinking about a new leader coming into the business. Although, the fish maybe "rotten" and potentially it was the original head of the business that 'rotted' first, culture is determined by so much more than just leadership. The business support systems, including leadership, ensure that the culture is reinforced.

I've worked with clients who have changed over from a toxic leader to a positive leadership influence. And unfortunately, the rotting fish doesn't always stop rotting just because a new head comes along. Unless they are able to influence change and enabled to make tough decisions, the fish may continue to rot. Let's explore the role of an effective leader in culture change.

Leading Transformative Culture Change

There is much research conducted into 'effective' leadership. Although many are coming close and make recommendations, no one has specifically determined the 'best' leader. However, much of the research is showing consistency in a few areas. When I ask the participants in our leadership programs, team building events, or culture development workshops, to describe their ideal leader, i.e. what would that ideal leader do, say and think? They come up with similar concepts to the research. The three most common elements are competence, vision and compassion.

People expect their leader to be *competent*. Let's be clear though, the expectations are not just having a competence in a technical field. If for example you are the founder, CEO, or team leader within an accounting firm, people expect you to have credibility within the accounting field. They expect you to be able to 'speak the language' of accountancy, but the competence that they are seeking is management and leadership competence, not accounting competence. This is really important to note because a lot of the time, people are promoted to leadership and management positions because of their technical competence. Unfortunately, technical competence does not determine if you are an effective leader or not. All technical competence does is give you credibility within a field of expertise. It may ensure that the people who report to you are confident that you can communicate with them effectively about their work and help them to make decisions. However, when they judge their leader, it's on management competencies like communication, feedback and decision making, not their technical skills.

Another element that people look for in their leaders is *inspiration and vision*. They want their leaders to have a vision for the future. They want to be able to follow that leader. An effective leader will be clear about the direction that they are heading. They will be able to communicate about the work output and how it contributes to the end result. They will be visionary and give their team something to aspire towards. They will be connected to the vision of the business, and will help their team to feel connected to it also.

> **People want to follow you, so you must know where you are heading.**

For example, an effective leader at Instagram will be demonstrably connected to their vision *"capturing and sharing the world's memories."* Let's say they are managing the payroll team through a continuous improvement activity. The team are 'technically' not capturing or sharing the memories directly, so the leader must be inspiring and visionary themselves to enable the connection. They may say, and demonstrate through their actions, how important it is to get the payroll efficient and have a low error rate. They will help their team to see that by improving the payroll systems and procedures, that the accuracy rate will increase, or perhaps will provide the capacity for additional services. These improvements mean that the rest of the business is not distracted by worrying about their pay check. They are focused on making improvements and providing a better user experience. By the payroll team being amazing at their job, the rest of the business can be amazing at theirs and thus support the vision.

As a leader, you need to be clear about where you are going, and you need to be able to clearly articulate the direction, because how can you be a leader if no one's following?

Research shows that the third thing people expect from an effective leader is *compassion*.

Unfortunately, when we're handed the role of leader or manager as a young professional, unless we've had great mentors or deliberate skills development, we think we are the Boss (with a capital B). The Boss is someone who rules over other people. Even if we're the kind of person that enjoys relationships, when we're first handed this management role and we're not also handed the skills, abilities and competencies along with it, we may take on a persona that we saw in our own bosses or we see on television. The role of the controlling, know-everything Boss is a popular archetype in modern media.

Don't be a Boss, be a leader.

What people are looking for in their leader is understanding. Just be human first. Just look your people in the eye. Treat them like you would treat anybody else. Speak to them like you would speak to a friend. Ask them questions, get to know them, understand that you have a role and they have a role to play. That together you have specific tasks that need to occur. You've got responsibilities, you have accountabilities in your role – as do they. And your specific accountability is to help them deliver on their accountabilities. Therefore, in fact, as a leader you serve your people.

Simon Sinek's book *Leaders Eat Last* explores the concept of servant leadership. In the book he examines the military's approach to leadership. The most fascinating thing that I found while reading this book, and reading other research about military leadership, is how much of the success of that leadership is due to a servant leadership approach.

It's quite counterintuitive because when you ask people about the defence forces, they think about the command and control approach. There's definitely an element of that, of course, and there are people within the organizations that behave that way. But the great military leader, when you examine how they lead, they're always human first. They provide an environment where their people can succeed. They care about their people and do what they need to do to ensure that every single soldier goes home safe at night. AND they make tough calls. They make the hard decisions so that they can provide an environment where all of their people succeed. Let's be clear, the servant leadership approach focuses on the human in the situation, but it is not a soft approach, it's not a pandering approach, and it's not weak.

In 1999, Australian General Peter Cosgrove famously led the East Timor peace keeping mission. He had 11,000 people in his care. He is known for his stern but fair approach and the focus he places on the privilege of great leadership. The more you discover about him the more it becomes obvious that he recognizes the need to not only be competent, but serve your people in a way that they can put their trust in you.

"It's instructive to consider the more spectacular and well-known falls from grace of leaders in the public eye... In the main, the issues behind these falls could be grouped under a lack of competence, a lack of support or loyalty from those they sought to lead, and a lack of failure of integrity. Of all these, the last is the most egregious, the most fatal. We so much want our leaders to be unfailingly decent that an obvious or perceived flaw in integrity can be the toxin which kills them off." – General Peter Cosgrove

A servant leader is focused on the individual, and balances that focus with the greater good.

If a servant leader has a team member who is not performing in their organization, they will manage the performance of that person. If they can help them to grow, learn and develop to become great at their job then that's what they will do. If the person cannot grow, develop and learn and become great in their role, then the servant leader will help them leave the organization. It's not just about serving one person when you're a leader. To be a truly great leader, and particularly a truly effective servant leader, there's a significant balancing act between holding the person to account while also recognizing that they're humans and they're fallible. While also recognizing that the whole team is affected by each individual member of the team, and that the outcomes for the ultimate customer needs to be considered. It's a holistic approach to leadership that produces the best results.

In the military, leaders can quite literally hold people's lives in their hands. A great leader must recognize that people are precious, that they are not yours to be bossed around or do the bidding of one person. Each and every person in the business or in your team, has a role to play and when one of them does not play their role, then the whole team suffers.

The role of the leader in changing culture is to be, first and foremost, an effective leader. It is to create an environment where change can happen. The role of the leader is not to change people because quite frankly that's not possible. You cannot change someone else. The only person you have control over changing is yourself. However, as a leader, you do have the influence and ability to control and change the environment that your people are working within. If you create an environment where change can happen, then change will happen. If you place barriers in the way, then change won't happen. If you don't address performance that is holding you back, then change won't happen. If you don't recognize when your people need a shoulder to lean on, then change won't happen.

Here are a few ways that a leader can influence culture change:

1. Making decisions – review all alternatives, evidence, and possible impacts before making big decisions. Make little decisions quickly, or better yet, delegate them all.
2. Setting expectations – ensure that the expectations are clear, people know how they are expected to behave and the resulting consequences.

3. Communicating – communicating is more than just sending an email, or giving a presentation at a team meeting. Great communication is engaging, honest and provided for the other person. It enables better results and makes people feel evolved in the process.
4. Process reviewing – challenge the current processes and find new ways that provide better outcomes, with greater efficiencies. You can save money and provide better results – you just have to ask the right questions and challenge the norms.
5. Teaching and supporting – teach others your technical skills so that your people can do the work, and you can grow as a leader. When you are the only expert in the room they'll always need you in that room. Not really conducive to progression… is it?

Key Take-away

A leader may not completely rot the culture, however the leader has a significant role to play in enabling culture to change. Their behavior influences how decisions are made, budgets are set, expectations are rewarded, people are held accountable, conversations are had, care is given, and collaboration happens.

Self-coaching Questions

- How can I serve my team, my business and my customer to get better results for all of us?

Chapter 5:
Culture is Everybody's Business

> *When people show you who they are, believe them. I carry that with me a lot. It has served me well."*
>
> Shonda Rhimes, writer and TV producer

"How you treat people when they leave your business, says more about your culture than how you treat people when they join." – Michelle T Holland

Chapter 5: Culture is Everybody's Business

Are you a culture warrior or a culture worrier?

A culture warrior is someone who works hard to create a culture that is going to deliver the best results for the customer and the people within the business. They question themselves, they question the systems, and they question the results, and they act and make improvement.

A culture worrier is someone who doesn't like the culture that they are currently working within, complains about it, talks about it, speaks about all the things that the business *should* do but they don't really do much about it themselves.

A warrior takes deliberate action; a worrier hopes that someone else will take deliberate action.

Worry is such a strange emotion. Without actions, worry becomes completely useless.

A number of years ago when I first started consulting, I had a period where I was struggling. I worried about the business, I worried about the sales, I worried about the messages I was sending to my kids, I worried what my friends and family thought, I worried… constantly. I was doing nothing for my health and wellbeing. I continued worrying until I saw a meme on Facebook. It's insane to think that one of those stupid memes changed my life… but it did.

The meme looked like this:

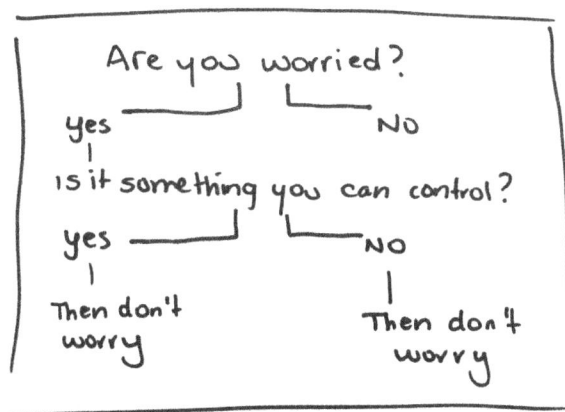

Are you worried?

yes ────────┘ └──── NO

is it something you can control?

yes ────────┘ └──── NO

Then don't worry

Then don't worry

There's no science to this, but it made me rethink how I was using my time. I realized by worrying about things I couldn't control, it took my energy. Worrying about things I could control took my power away. I started to take action on the elements I could control and release the things I couldn't. Now, when I begin to worry, I access my inner Warrior (or Slayer if you've read my other book – *Energy Vampires Suck*) and I take action.

We are all responsible for our own life experiences. If you are worried about your culture, think about what action you CAN take, not the action you can't.

Business culture is made up of the collective – the collective values, experiences, actions and activities of all the individuals within the business. Without thinking that you impact on the culture and that you can be the solution… then we're in trouble straight away.

The biggest mistake that people make is in thinking that they can't do anything to change the culture and by doing so render themselves powerless. This is the worry of the culture worrier. The culture warrior is quite different. The culture warrior finds actions that they can take. They *believe* that change is possible.

Below are a few questions to see where you are right now on the spectrum of culture worrier or the culture warrior. Ideally you want to be a culture warrior. Ideally we want everyone in the business to be a culture warrior. This is because for true change to happen, it must start with each individual.

Culture Worrier or Warrior?

For each question give yourself a score out of ten. On a spectrum, ten means that you fully engage in this behavior daily and the people you work with would happily confirm this score. One means that you never or rarely engage in the behavior.

1. I have conversations with my peers about the outcomes of their decisions.
2. I take long term and short term actions that enable the best outcome for my customer and my team.
3. I say hello and smile to people that I meet in the elevator, pass in the hallway or in the kitchen.
4. I understand the impact of my work and systems on others in the business and work to eliminate negative impacts.
5. I believe in the business's vision and know-how my contribution helps to achieve that future.
6. I genuinely care about the people I work with and it saddens me when they are not performing at their best.
7. I challenge myself and my peers to create better ways of working.

8. I have challenging conversations with my peers and leaders about how performance outcomes can be improved.
9. I know my peers and my leaders well and ask them about their hopes, dreams, aspirations and future direction.
10. I work daily to create improvements in the work that I do.

If you have scored less than 55 then you are probably a culture worrier, between 55 and 75 you are heading in the right direction, and over 75… carry on culture warrior!

You'll notice that these statements have a balance between getting outcomes and caring for people. Of course this is not a scientific survey, it's just a quick way to reflect on the role that you are playing in the activity of culture. The score is not important, what is really important is to analyze why you didn't score yourself a zero or a ten in any of the statements. If you did score a zero, then you may want to get some help to look into why. It's in the why question that you will find the gold for creating a great culture. Like any survey, the score is meaningless if you do nothing other than focus on the score. Debating the questions and the score becomes a distraction and in many cases is actually work avoidance. The important take away from this is to recognize that you have a role to play in creating the culture you have now and a role to play in creating the culture that you want.

The role that the individual plays in culture development is significant because we each have an impact even if we think we don't. If you believe you are a victim and have no impact, you are actually having a huge impact because of that belief. The biggest impact a person can have is believing they are powerless. You become an anchor for the culture warrior who is trying to move swiftly and create change. If they are always having to slow down to check on you and make sure you feel secure in the change then you are slowing them down. Stand up and take control of your own powerlessness and you'll change the culture.

The culture is everybody's business. It's not just the leaders. Although the leader, as we discussed in the previous chapter, has quite a significant role to play. However, the leader or leaders won't be able to change the culture completely without the role of the individual.

Let's get real though… you have a role to play, but as an individual you're not going to be able to change *everything*. If the executive leadership team are causing big problems, then as an individual staff member you may have limited opportunities to be able to change it. You can't change everything, but you can change the areas you are responsible for, and you can change how you behave in response to the culture.

You've probably noticed that worriers and warriors display their behavior in different ways. Understanding the role that we play in culture creation helps us to create a level playing ground and enable culture transformation. It allows us to examine our own contribution so we're not shifting blame. By understanding these roles or archetypes it can help you bring others along on the culture journey by speaking their language.

Cultural Archetypes

We take on many roles in life. Many are useful and helpful, like mother, father, carer, cook, lover etc. Many roles are not helpful and can create problems in your life and your relationships. Roles like criticizer, worrier and yeller.

When it comes to creating a business through culture; your people – and you – will take on various roles which at times can be helpful and other times… not. The role that you take on is influenced considerably by your personality, values, experiences and expectations. After many years of observing people within change I created eight archetypes to explain the roles that people play. I have briefly described these archetypes to assist you to bring your people along for the ride.

The Imagineer
The Analyser
The Dreamer
The Resourcer
The Teacher
The Doer
The Empathiser
The Regulator
Cutlure Inc
Archetypes

You may recognize yourself or your team mates in these roles. If you think that this is something that will help you in your culture journey please head over to synergyiq.com.au/bookbonuses to download a free video series that provides more detail about the Culture Archetypes, and how you can manage your interactions with them.

The Empathizer

How to recognize them
The empathizer is an emotional thinker and doer. They will make emotional decisions and talk about feelings.

How they help
They help by communicating to their colleagues and they also keep an eye on others in the team.

How they may hinder
They may get over emotional about the changes and quite fearful.

How to get them on board
Be honest and compassionate. Talk with them early and often about impact and how it will be managed.

The Teacher

How to recognize them
Like the empathizer they will use emotive language but it will be more future focused. They will also use language to heal situations and explore the future.

How they help
They will be the ones that help other people understand the impact of the change.

How they may hinder
They may get wrapped up in communication and fail to take action.

How to get them on board
Ensure that they have enough information, early on, to ensure that they are able to contribute to the conversation.

The Dreamer

How to recognize them
The dreamer is the one in the team that constantly has new ideas, perhaps gets bored or distracted easily in meetings.

How they help
They will be enthusiastic about the change and help others see the potential opportunities within the changes.

How they may hinder
They may get distracted with many new ideas and fail to implement the changes required.

How to get them on board
Allow them to provide ideas for the change.

The Imagineer

How to recognize them
They are the ones in your team who consistently have 'thinking face'. The imagineer will provide research and facts to back up their ideas.

How they help
They will provide critical thinking about what is likely to happen, and offer solutions.

How they may hinder
If they don't believe in the change or believe that the change is stupid, they may dismiss your ideas and the ideas of others.

How to get them on board
Allow them time to analyze the change and provide their thoughts and alternative ideas.

The Analyzer

How to recognize them
These are the members of your team who ask critical questions, all the time.

How they help
They will see gaps in the process or systems and allow you to find ways to prevent failure.

How they may hinder
They aren't great at being an agile team player so you'll see some resistance to new ideas that are not theirs.

How to get them on board
Ensure they understand the need for change and have access to detailed information regarding this need.

The Resourcer

How to recognize them
They are focused on how they can get action happening and how they can contribute to the change.

How they help
They will source resources and document project plans and do it within budget.

How they may hinder
They may appear resistant to change, particularly at first.

How to get them on board
They are usually great planners so get them involved in drafting the plans, or at least sense checking them.

The Doer

How to recognize them
These are the action oriented members of your team who just get on with it.

How they help
They will keep your projects on track and make sure deadlines are met.

How they may hinder
During change, they generally the most resistant group and will make the change but begrudgingly.

How to get them on board
Be really clear with them about their role in the change.

The Regulator

How to recognize them
They are the ones in your team who like structure and rules because it makes them feel safe.

How they help
They are fantastic at assessing change impact on people and processes.

How they may hinder
They may become very emotional and negative during change.

How to get them on-board
Be straight with them and honest about the impact the change will have on them.

There you go, eight different archetypes that you will come across in the workplace and life. Of course, we all are able to behave within each of these types, but generally we will sway towards one or two naturally. Observe your teammates and the people across the organization to see how these types play out.

Now that you have an understanding of the various roles people play you are able to use this information to assist you when you are developing your culture plan and your communication strategy. You must avoid labelling people though because you may inadvertently create an environment whereby people cannot grow. Understand the role, and understand how you can manage these roles and help people grow beyond them.

Creating the culture you want, or changing a culture you don't want is possible, you just need the skills, resources and knowhow. The next part of the book will tell you how.

Key Take-away

Culture is everyone's responsibility. Don't wait for someone else to act so you can enjoy a better day at work.

> ### Self-coaching Questions
>
> • How do the culture archetypes play out in my workplace? How do I demonstrate the culture that we want? How can I be a culture warrior more often?

Part 2:

Creating Change

MEASURE → ANALYZE → PLAN → ACT → (cycle back to MEASURE)

Part 2: Creating Change

Just before finalizing this book I was working with a large utility company to help them change their culture. It's a business bound by rules and regulations, and they know they need to transform to get better outcomes for their customers. They recognized the need for change, but they were still struggling to make change.

This became evident when I was meeting with one of their skilled business leaders. We were discussing how to create a new culture when I saw the penny suddenly drop for her…

"Do you think people know what it takes to change culture...really? Do you think they know this (pointing to the whiteboard) is a huge part of it?" she asked.

My answer was no, many don't, not yet.

"But we've been talking about culture and our ideal culture for years, why don't they know?"

My short but honest answer was, because most people don't want to do what it takes to transform a business. They are focused on the behavior training and the individual and forget about the collective way we reinforce behaviors and actions.

Many business leaders are struggling to understand the work needed to change… including many of the change, culture and HR professionals who have been left in charge of it. They understand the theory behind it and some of them even know a 'change management process', but for many people the penny is yet to drop.

What my experience shows me is that eventually the people in the business understand that culture is important (step 1 – tick), then they come to understand the desired state on an intellectual level (step 2 – tick), and then they start behavior training programs for their staff (step 3….?), and then… well in many businesses step 4 ends up being a repeat of steps 1–3.

The training didn't work. So what is a manager to do but… blame the individual staff member and the consultant/trainer, or believe that people still don't understand the need for culture, or introduce a new measurement tool because clearly the last one didn't work to change the culture? And then the merry-go-round starts again.

A number of clients that I have worked with are somewhere on this merry-go-round and my job is to get them off and onto a new track that will lead them to where they need to be. This is the most challenging part of my job. Many business leaders don't know what to do, but are averse to asking for help because of their ego. They believe that they should know what to do because they are a leader. Interestingly, they wouldn't hesitate to call in an expert if they needed to fix their plumbing or electricity, but many leaders are hesitant to ask for an expert to support them through a transformation program.

Culture, change and business transformation is a specialised skill so don't be worried about buying it in if you need to, even if you think it's part of your job and you think you 'should' know. A willingness to actually change the work that you are doing, and get expert support when needed, shows maturity and a transformation mindset. To identify and change the structures that hold the culture exactly where it is takes time and the skill.

Ironically, most businesses describe culture as 'the way we do things around here' – this description is, as we know, only part of the culture story, but golly... even if you just believed this then how can you miss the fact that culture changes through changing 'the way' of working?

Johann Hari, in his book *Lost Connections*, argues that depression is misunderstood. One of the arguments he makes is that not enough attention is given to the way society functions and its impact on depression. When he made this argument I couldn't help but make the correlation with culture in organizations. Often the individual is 'blamed' or expected to change, without the support of the organization. They talk about empowerment, decision making and engagement like they are independent to the business systems and leadership.

Why do we make it hard for people to be the best versions of themselves?

For an individual to change they must take responsibility for themselves and their actions. They, if resilient and determined, will make change regardless of the circumstances. Viktor Frankl's story, *Man's Search for Meaning*, clearly showed us that positive change can occur even in the worst of circumstances. He said, "Anything can be taken from a man but one thing: the last of the human freedoms – to choose one's own attitude in any given set of circumstances, to choose one's own way."

There's no denying people CAN make change in hard circumstances. The question is, couldn't there be a better way? Do we have to go through terrible things to change? Struggle is important to growth, but when the struggle is too hard the benefits can be lost. People may start a change process and find that the struggle against the system is too much and they stop.

Do you want to see your people succeeding despite your business environment, or because of it?

If you can shift your culture so that all of the people who want to make change, can make change without a massive struggle, why wouldn't you?

Successful business transformation happens through deliberate and holistic action, not by accident, and definitely not by leaving it up to the individual to 'just behave differently'.

Believe that change is possible, and join me as I introduce you to my methodology for culture change. *FORM, FLOW and FEEL*.

Chapter 6:
The Will and the Way

"Learn what is true in order to do what is right."

Thomas Huxley

"The question unasked, is the question left unanswered." – Michelle T Holland

Chapter 6: The Will and the Way

Essentially there are three mental stages to change. The first stage is acknowledgement, then acceptance, and then finally action. Unfortunately we humans jump the gun and head straight for action before really understanding the root cause and accepting it.

I'm going to show you a powerful and effective way of making your business a better place to work and do business. Before you use this system you need the will to make change. You'll have to acknowledge the problems you may be facing in your business. You need to acknowledge where the problems are coming from. This process can be challenging, because sometimes the biggest problem in your business…. is you…

A good way to start this process is to use an impartial method of assessing the culture and your leadership style. There are many tools out there to do this. You should choose one that suits you and delivers the benefits that you need. On synergyiq.com.au website there is a resource that helps you understand the different types of tools and how to select the best one for you.

I generally use a diagnostic process which tells you how your business is performing, what the gaps are, what your people are interested in and what they're not, and what strategies are having an impact and what is not. The data that you get from diagnostic tools, such as the ones I use, are brilliant. The information provides a clear guide about your culture. It gives you an indication of where you're getting traction with actions, and where you're not.

These tools provide you with information about where you are right now. Unfortunately there are many business leaders that once they ask the question they hide the data away because they don't like what it says. I was told by a colleague that their CEO hid the data set in his bottom drawer. He didn't want the managers to see the outcome. Unfortunately, this is not uncommon.

My advice to you if this sounds familiar is STOP WASTING TIME AND MONEY MEASURING CULTURE IF YOU AREN'T GOING TO DO ANYTHING WITH IT. I've capitalised that so you hear it, and so the people around you can hear it. There is honestly nothing worse than asking your employees for their opinions and then ignoring them. It's a very quick way to break trust and disengage a group of people.

The businesses that I've worked with who have been successful in culture change are the ones that take the data seriously.

However I've also worked with companies in the past, where no matter how much guidance you provide them, they still don't want to use the data the way the data needs to be used.

Many organizations run surveys but they don't dig deep enough into the data. They take it on face value. For example, the culture data comes back and says that the employees are not satisfied in the work that they are currently doing. So they say "We need to come up with some mechanism for satisfying the employees" when they should be saying "What is the fundamental cause of the dissatisfaction?"

Business leaders aren't asking 'why' enough. I often joke with people that I'm just like a four-year-old child, because I ask so many questions. The main question that I ask is 'why?' Why do the results say your people aren't engaged? Why aren't your people in finance staying more than two years? Why is your performance management system failing? Why are people not connected to the vision?

Just keep asking why until you get to the root cause.

It's not enough to find out what the data is saying, you must find out why it is saying what it's saying. Using a why, why, why, why approach is often the best. If you ask why enough, you'll eventually get to the end result.

One of my clients introduced a 'quick culture check survey'. They run a brief survey every quarter to get a sense of how people are feeling. It's a very simplistic tool whereby the data they receive is more interesting than enabling, however, the brilliance of the tool is the conversation that people are having when they're filling out the survey.

You see, this survey gives them an immediate response. The person filling in the survey can see how they are feeling within the context of their culture. This immediate return stops people from being able to say, "Well, I'm fine. It's all those bastards over there. They have a problem with this organization. But I'm great." It also enables people who do feel great about the organization to talk about why. People are having conversations around what motivation is, what engagement means, what it means to be satisfied at work, and what others do to stay motivated/ engaged/satisfied.

Many basic surveys essentially ask questions to get an answer to one question – "Do they like working here?"

This is great to know. If people say yes then you can assume that your business is doing the right things and doesn't need to change. If they say no then you can assume that they are just whingers and should leave the business…. see where I'm going with this? There actually isn't enough information in this answer to make any realistic assumptions at all. Remember what they say about assume… it make an ASS out of U and ME.

Without digging deep into what the culture is saying about the systems, the behavior, the processes, decision making, or the leadership, regardless about how somebody's feeling on a day-to-day basis, we're not going to get the kind of change that we want.

I think this is one of the main reasons why businesses tend to measure the data and then put it on a shelf and not look at it again. It is because the information from this data is hard to deal with. If the data tells you that your employees are not motivated, what does that mean for you as a business leader?

As a business leader, it is not your responsibility to motivate your employees. It is not your responsibility to make your employees happy. It is not your responsibility to make the people around you satisfied in their work.

What the hell? Michelle has lost her mind…

I know this is very different than what you've been told in the past. As a business leader you have been made to believe that if your people are unhappy or unmotivated then it's all your fault, and you are a bad manager. Well, that is not necessarily true. Yes, you need to take responsibility for the environment that you are creating. If you are constantly yelling, or putting people down, or taking their work away from them, or not making decisions, then yes your people may experience less satisfaction because of these things. You are responsible for the environment you create, but you are not responsible for their reaction to it. You cannot in any way make someone behave differently, make someone happy or make someone sad. They have control over their behavior and emotion… not you.

For those of you who reading this and have young children, you know this for a fact. You know you cannot make another human being do anything that they don't want to. You can influence, you can ask, you can cajole, you can bribe but you cannot *make* them do something that they do not want to do. You can threaten; you can abuse, you could hold a gun to the person's head, and still that person has a choice. If they choose to do what you say, they will only ever do *exactly* what you tell them to do and nothing more, because their motivation is to stop the pain, not to please you.

I don't want you to read this and feel like you're off the hook because as a business leader, you have an extremely important role to play in the motivation factors of your people. If your people are lacking motivation, engagement, satisfaction and don't intend to be around for a very long time, you need to take this seriously. You will need to examine what is actually causing the problems you are seeing. You need to dig deep and discover the cause prior to creating a solution. This is why you need to have the will to change, not just the way to change. Leadership is a tough gig, particularly in times of struggle and change… but it's also a privilege because you are able to help your team be the best they can be. What an honor it is to see one of your team flourishing because of the support you give them.

As a leader you are responsible for supporting them in reaching their full potential. Which means getting them help when they need it, creating the environment in which they work and being careful about the selection of the people that they work with.

You are also responsible for the processes and the systems, resources and tools, and assessing the skill development that they need to get their job done. You are responsible for setting the expectations for them so they know what job you want them to do. Nowhere in this are you responsible for their happiness or their motivation.

Happiness and motivation comes from within a person... period.

Culture is not happiness. An outcome of a positive and effective organizational culture is sometimes happiness. More often, it's satisfaction.

Let's explore the word 'satisfaction' just for a moment, shall we? We talk about employee satisfaction quite a bit and occasionally we replace the word satisfaction with happiness or engagement. I've heard people define happy at work as – people who don't complain, people who just turn up and do their job, people that are happy through change. They are happy when their business leader provides a new entitlement for them, or gives them a pay rise.

When we define satisfaction as happiness we can get disappointed fast. Happiness is completely subjective. You can have a group of passive and compliant people, who are very happy. If happiness is your goal, then great, but if you also want quality results and outcomes then sometimes that is in conflict with happiness.

Satisfaction in the workplace is just that – satisfaction – the fulfillment of one's expectations or needs. Its baseline stuff, it's not a driver for greatness. So, let's not tie ourselves in knots over satisfaction. Yes it's an outcome that we want from a culture transformation, but it's not the only one and it's definitely not a strong enough driver for change.

If we always aim for mediocrity, we'll always get there.

If we only ever measure satisfaction, of course, we will only ever set a bar at 'good'.

We want to be setting the bar a lot higher. The first line in Jim Collins' popular book *Good to Great – Why some companies make the leap and others don't*, is "Good is the enemy to great." I love this line because it challenges people who are settled, who are satisfied and challenges them to do more and be more.

You want to be the best employer for people within the category in which you employ. If you are an IT developer and you want to recruit the best IT developers around, then you are competing against Google and Atlassian. They have great cultures and they go beyond the call of duty for their employees because they don't set the bar at satisfaction.

If you are only collecting satisfaction or engagement data and you aren't seeing the change you want, then perhaps it's time to dig deeper. When you review culture data that is mined using a robust and researched methodology, it will still require analysis and questions, but you will be able to ask smarter questions and get to the causation issues a lot quicker.

If it is your goal to be a business with a high performing and engaged workforce that delivers great results for your customer and that earns a substantial profit while doing it, then you need to set the bar above satisfaction.

First you measure, then you analyze, then you plan, and then you create a goal, then you act, and then you measure again, and then you analyze again, and then you review/modify the plan and the goal, and then you act again. And it's a continual cycle of change. It's a continual cycle of testing and re-testing, measuring and re-measuring.

"It's very important to have a feedback loop, where you constantly think about how you could be doing things better and questioning yourself."
– Elon Musk, Entrepreneur and Founder, Tesla and SpaceX

Don't waste your time and money asking questions, diagnosing your culture, figuring out your engagement scores, looking at your key performance indicators (KPIs), if you're not going to do anything with that data. It's a waste of time, it's a waste of money, it's a waste of energy. And actually what it does is it sets up expectations with your employees which deteriorates trust. If you want a quick way to disengage your workforce and negatively affect your culture then run surveys and do nothing with the data.

Data and information about your current reality is essential to enable you to create a plan that will address the areas within your business that are affecting the form, flow and feel of your business.

Key Take-away

By using an integrated strategy and integrated approach to measurement and change, you can change your organizations. It's not a wand, and there is no magic potion. It's just a simple formula of collecting data, diagnosing, understanding root cause, and effort. And if you're willing to do that, then you're willing to change your culture.

Self-coaching Questions

- How can I get more out of the data we currently collect?
- How can I hold myself and my business accountable for creating change?
- How can I assess if our business leaders are willing to do what it takes to change the culture?

Chapter 7:
FORM – Start with a Strong Foundation

> *"Good leaders organize and align people around what the team needs to do. Great leaders motivate and inspire people with why they're doing it. That's purpose. And that's the key to achieving something truly transformational."*
>
> Marillyn Hewson, CEO
> Lockheed Martin

"Company values define what your company stands for, your personal values guide your thinking and behavior. When they align, magic happens."
– Michelle T Holland

Chapter 7: FORM – Start with a Strong Foundation

We can appreciate individual change. We've all tried to change something in our lives. Maybe it was learning to stop smoking, or lose weight, or start speaking up in meetings.

In simple terms, the way to change business culture, on a long-term and sustainable basis, is that every individual in that business creates change in themselves and subsequently creates the changes needed in the way the business functions. Simple huh?

There are a ton of experts in individual change. Plenty of YouTube channels devoted to 'being your best you'. I'm not trying to be flip, because working on self is a critical component to society and company change. But the complexities of collective change warrant more thought and a different skill set, which is why I created the FORM, FLOW and FEEL methodology.

The methodology allows managers, business leaders, CEOs and founders to identify and change the critical elements of their business, while also working on themselves.

I want to ensure that you have the resources, the capability and the capacity to be able to create change yourself. I know you can do it.

I work with some extraordinary companies and extraordinary people who are very, very capable. The reason they call me in is because my team and I have skills in a specialty areas that they don't, i.e. business transformation. By working together we achieve the result they want. By teaching them how, they can stay the course – the 'teach a man to fish' philosophy.

Let me introduce you to the model that I use with my clients.

Culture is the *FORM, FLOW and FEEL* of the business.

To start, let me ask you a question.
What is at the heart of a great business?

Many people will say customers. Some will say its people are at the heart. Others might highlight the leaders or the founder's vision. They are all correct. The heart of every successful business is a strong foundation that allows the leaders and people to flourish so that they can serve the customer.

How you think about that question will largely depended on what your bias is. If you are a business finance manager then you'll think about the budgets and actuals first. If you are the HR Manager you'll probably think about the people first, marketing is customers, engineering is the project plan, sales people is the sales. We all have the capacity and capability to think beyond our specialty and many do, but generally our bias rules our first thoughts and that's ok, as long as you work as a team and don't rely solely on your own ideas.

The foundation stones of a business guide how we think about the outcomes we are working to achieve, and how we conduct ourselves while we are working. They are the baseline principles and expectations that set us up for success or for failure.

When we're talking about individual change, we talk about mindset and identity. These are the foundations of creating lasting personal change. If I believe that I am a person who doesn't exercise and that's what I fundamentally believe about myself, then it is going to be very hard to stick to an exercise routine.

Businesses work in a similar way. If we believe we have a low tolerance for risk and we establish procedures, policies and structures that demonstrate this low tolerance for risk, then it will be difficult to suddenly become an organization of innovation which is risky business. The identity that your business has, must be supported by its foundations.

When you form a business you begin with the foundation stones.

FORM

FEEL

FLOW

The FORM part of the puzzle – the foundation stones

To transform your business, start by analyzing the FORM elements of culture:

- The vision – is it clear, inspiring and provides a future direction?
- The mission/strategy – do people understand the purpose of the work and the critical outcomes and objectives?
- The values and behavior – do your people understand what the business stands for and how you want them to behave to produce the results you want to achieve?
- The leadership/governance – is it clear, from the top down to the bottom up, what best practice means, where the business is heading, and how you are getting there?

- Customers/community – do we know who they are and what they want, and are we in a position to deliver to the standard that they need? How do we give back to them?

Creating strong foundation stones for your business means that your culture can be built and won't fall down in the first storm.

Let's start working on your foundation stones.

Key foundation stone 1 – Vision
The vision of a business is an inspirational statement to tell people where the business is heading. It allows people to be inspired. It gives them direction. It's essentially the destination, but as we know, the fun happens in the journey not the destination. Another way to think about it is that when the business has achieved everything it sets out to do, this is the ultimate outcome. The vision is generally very aspirational and long term, it's the big picture dream of the business.

Here are examples of great vision statements from successful businesses:

- Life is Good (t-shirts) – *Spread the power of optimism*
- IKEA (furniture) – *A better everyday life for the many people*
- Zappos (online retail) – *Delivering happiness to customers, employees, and vendors*
- Disney (entertainment) – *To make people happy*
- Google (search engine) – *To organize the world's information and make it universally accessible and useful*
- Harley-Davidson (motorcycles) – *To fulfil dreams through the experiences of motorcycling*
- Instagram (online photo-sharing) – *Capture and share the world's moments*

As we can see with these vision statements, they are inspiring and broad. Zappos say they are in business to deliver happiness… not shoes. Life is Good are in it for the optimism, they just happen to sell t-shirts.

Instagram is a social media platform, but they want to help people share *moments*. These statements are something that people can connect to and want to be a part of. A vision statement evokes emotion.

Jim Collins calls big picture inspirational goals, BHAGs. I like to think of the vision as a BHAG – a Big, Hairy, Audacious Goal. It's not something that's going to be reached tomorrow. It's not something that's even going to be reached next week or next year.

Google have a reputation for having a great culture and many of you may have said "I'd love to work for Google." We hear a lot about the lunch rooms, the bean bags and how cool the Googleplex is, but there's more to Google's culture than just the free food and gym memberships. People work for Google because of what they stand for and are working towards. Google's vision statement is very specific to them, but is not so specific that it becomes part of the strategy. This vision statement guides their decisions. If they want to achieve greatness, they must employ great people with great skills, therefore an action they take to support the vision is to have an appealing work environment.

People don't go and work for Google because they are a conventional company. People work for Google because they are constantly challenging the status quo. They are challenging the way in which they do business and they challenge how people obtain knowledge. When you think about the purpose of Google and what they've actually delivered to the world, it's easy to attribute meaning to the work that they do. Quite simply, Google has allowed everyone to have access to the collective knowledge of the planet. It's quite an astonishing feat.

Google's vision statement says not only what they do, but it talks about how big their goal is – the world's knowledge. Clearly, there's a lot of information on Google already and yet that's not the world's knowledge. When you dig further into Google's vision it's not just about collecting knowledge, but it's also about how all people can access it (universally accessible). We all know that knowledge and education are critical components of inclusion and equity. The human race won't progress until everyone, regardless of birthplace, has the same ability to learn as all others. When you break down this vision it is highly ambition and heart based. I don't even work for Google and could happily stand behind this vision.

How do you create a vision like this for your business?

Generally, a good place to start is with the "We believe...<fill in the blanks>..." approach

Synergy IQ's vision statement is *"To challenge the status quo and inspire growth, so that people feel valued and companies become great."* This vision has come from my personal belief that every person deserves to feel valued in their workplace and must be valued for their unique contribution. This belief is deep for me and therefore for my business. Having our belief in our vision means that the people I work with believe in the vision and demonstrate it through their behavior. If they didn't believe it, then they wouldn't work with me. It's as simple as that. It also allows me to be discerning about the clients that I work with. This is why a vision is important. Don't have one if it's a cookie cut vision that is everything to everyone. It becomes completely invalid and a waste of time if your vision statement is not divisive.

To create your own belief based vision statement, start with answering the following questions and then determine a short statement that includes the essence of what you have answered:

1. What do I fundamentally believe as the founder/CEO/Managing Director?

2. What are my non-negotiables? That is, I won't back down on these issues no matter what.
3. When I think about the past, what am I most proud of that we've achieved as a business, and why?
4. When I look to the past, what failures stand out the most, and why?
5. How does this business change the lives of others?
6. How does the business stand apart for other businesses in the same sector?
7. What are the things my people tell me that they are most proud of within this business or of the achievements of the business?

Look at your answers and find the common belief-based elements. Once you see the common elements then determine if they are the elements that you want your business to be known for, if they are then do some wordsmithing and come up with a statement that is short, inspiring and future focused. Test this statement with a number of people and allow them to provide you feedback. Modify it based on the feedback if you think the feedback adds value.

You will end up with a short statement that will generally be structured like this:

"What we do, and why we do it."

If the answers you have provided to the questions above are demonstrating a business, behavior or beliefs that you do not want to be known for, or you find it offensive, then you've got some serious transformation work to do… and it starts with creating a new vision and supporting the new vision with new values.

The next step of the process is to determine who you want to be known as when you are engaged in the process of obtaining your vision.

Foundation stone 2 – Values

Values are a foundation stone because they influence the FORM, the FLOW and the FEEL of the business. Values are what a business stands for, the values are what they want to be recognized for above all else. If the vision is the goal, and the strategy is what we need to do to reach the vision, then the values represent who we are (as a collective), and influence how we behave along the way.

Company values help you reach your goal because they support the value proposition for your customers, and they guide the way people think and act.

Another way of thinking about it is this, the company values are what the company values. Your personal values, are what you personally value. When they are in alignment then you will feel loyalty and a sense of connected purpose, and they (the company, and your personal values) will guide how you behave. Note I said alignment…they don't have to be the same.

Let's think about it this way – you're in Chicago and want to get to San Francisco. Your friend gives you directions which takes you to Los Angeles. Let's say you follow the directions without questioning them or thinking about them, big surprise, you end up in Los Angeles. Now Los Angeles is a lovely place, but it's not the destination you are aiming for. The value that you are demonstrating is compliance, i.e. not rocking the boat and not having a conflict.

Let's overlay a different set of values. Let's say your company values are about creating better ways, communication and curiosity, and that you align with these values – i.e. you were selected for this business because you share similar values. On your way to San Francisco you'll start noticing things that don't seem quite right. You'll allow your curiosity to explore why those things don't seem quite right. You'll figure out that there are landmarks along the way that don't appear to be taking you to San Francisco and eventually, you'll look very closely at the directions and see that they're taking you to Los Angeles. At that point, you'll talk to the other people in the car and tell them that you're going in the wrong direction, and because you are innovative and looking for better ways, together you'll figure out how you can get to San Francisco.

Your vision may give you direction, but without clear values, you could head off track. You may develop a reputation that you don't want. Your business might not stand for what you believe in and may not deliver what you actually want to deliver. If you want to be a specific kind of company, then your values have to align, and so do the people.

Zappos is a great example of a values-led business. Zappos CEO Tony Hsieh established a culture that drives performance in his business. He believes that it drives the outcomes that he wants. It drives the experience that his customers have. He was deliberate in setting up that culture by being clear about the values and behaviors that he wants every single employee of Zappos to demonstrate. Zappos has been explicit about their ten key values and they've been clear that this is the cornerstone of their culture. They live their values. Personally, I think there's too many of them and plus they are more 'behavior statements' than values, but it works for Zappos. I believe it works for Zappos because they are the focus of the business and the foundation stone of their strategy.

This is the key point; your values must work for you. Zappos values are embedded in everything Zappos does. It's not about the words... it's about how those words are demonstrated daily by employees and managers.

There's a business based in Sydney, Australia called *The Entourage*. The Entourage work to create great entrepreneurs. They help business leaders through education in the entrepreneurial space. The CEO of The

Entourage, Jack Delosa, is explicit about his personal values and shows conviction within them. Not surprising that the business' values and his values as CEO, are one in the same. This is not unusual, particularly with a Founder CEO.

When he recruits new people for his business, he's very clear that if you don't align directly to the values of The Entourage, you will not work there. He works to make sure that every single person that comes into The Entourage is extraordinarily clear about what is expected of them. Delosa is clear that their values and the business culture drives performance and the customer experience, and given his net value grew to 24 million three short years after starting The Entourage, he'd be pleased with the outcome.

Most businesses I work with generally have a set of 'values' or 'behavior' statements or words that they have printed on posters or up on their website. After reviewing the vision I look to the values to understand the kind of business they are.

The following information is structured under the most common questions that I hear when I'm working with clients to redesign their values.

What words should we use?

We are talking about corporate values. Many people get corporate values mixed up with individuals' values. This means you will see corporate values which have words like integrity, trust and respect, without a clear explanation of what they mean to the company. There is an assumption made that these generic values are what 'everyone' should display. If that's the case, then why pick them?

What we want is to have a set of corporate values that represents the business and to select people whose personal values align directly with the business. Corporate values aren't necessarily traditional words like 'trust'. This is a traditional value, a personal value, a common value. It's expected that most people value trust, whereas something like creativity may be less commonly held. It's not terrible to choose 'trust' if that is essential for your business, it's just less effective when you pick common held values for your business because they become meaningless if they are too vanilla.

A corporate value might be something like 'accountability' or 'creativity'.

Accountability is not a word that people would generally call a value, but when you think about accountability, it has trust, integrity and honestly embedded within the word. You have to be able to trust people to enable them to do their work and hold them accountable without micromanaging. Personal values are essentially embedded within corporate values or implied within corporate values.

By using words that are meaningful for your business you are able to communicate what your business actually stands for, while still allowing people to find their personal values embedded within the values and feel aligned to the business.

Using personal values can also set your business up for failure and judgement if you are not careful. Honesty is a good example. It's often used in codes of conduct and values lists because you want your people to be honest – however, remember the values are not just for the employees but also how the business is judged. When a corporation says that they are honest, you can almost guarantee that they are not living that value on a day-to-day basis, which leaves them open to being seen as disingenuous. Think about the way a corporation works – i.e. the accounting system, the tax system, the reporting system, the recruitment systems, etc. – these systems don't always lend themselves to honesty. It's not to say the people working within the business aren't honest, that isn't the point. The problem is you can't always be completely honest when you're working in a corporation because you report information strategically to make sure that the business reputation is maintained.

If you're in business, you know what I'm talking about. You know that you don't report absolutely everything that happens. You know that there are elements of your business that you keep just for yourself and just for your staff, that you don't want your customers to know about, that you don't want your public shareholders to know about. And it's not to say that you're not working with integrity. It may just be that if a customer knew absolutely everything about your business, there may be misunderstandings which impact your business.

> *"We are honest" (well most of the time, except in our annual report where we make it look good for shareholders, or when we talk to the media and leave out the negative stuff that goes on sometimes, or when... well, you can't expect honesty all the time for Pete's sake!)* - Company XYZ Values

We know that the media grabs hold of information from businesses and takes it completely out of context so it's no surprise that businesses are strategic about what they release. Just think about Starbucks' experience. Howard Schultz in his book *Onwards* disclosed a memo that he wrote to his management team which essentially said "We're not doing what we need to do to be successful and we need to change." The memo was leaked to the media who ran with a tantalizing story that 'revealed' that Starbucks was in big trouble and management were divided… their stock price took a hit for this story. Is it any wonder that many businesses want to keep their information carefully guarded?

When businesses have personal values as their company values, it becomes difficult for them to actually live their values.

Another example of what not to do, is one from a government department that I was reviewing recently. Not unlike many organizations, this department had 'innovative' as a value. The department enabled innovation in the community but it rarely innovated itself. Again, it's not to say the people working there aren't innovative. There are a lot of very bright people that work for the government that have a good understanding of innovation, have the capacity for innovation, and may be innovative within their sphere of influence.

Unfortunately there is so much bureaucracy and risk aversion due to the political environment, that they can't be truly innovative. Innovation requires risk taking, the ability to fail big, and to move fast. As Mark Zuckerberg has famously said to the people who work for Facebook "Move fast and break things." Private businesses have the luxury to do this, governments don't because of the public scrutiny and media attention – the Politian's want to be re-elected and 'breaking things' usually doesn't bode well for them.

Let's be clear, I'm not saying don't use innovation, unless you are Facebook, just be careful of what you are setting yourself up for when choosing the words you choose. Ask yourself "What is the evidence that we are X or Y?" and "What would our customer say if we asked them?"

How do I make generic words our own?

When you are creating your business values, there should be a descriptor about what you mean by the value. This is so that people are consistent in their application of the values and are not frightened off by them. Innovative is one that is commonly used across corporations and public sector organizations so I'll continue to use it to describe this point.

Take a private organization that is disrupting an industry, Uber for example – their value could easily include 'innovative' because they are literally innovating the way in which you get a ride; they have come up with a new method and created a new industry. This is an innovative approach. Other businesses may be better off having 'continuous improvement' instead of innovation because actually that's how they're defining innovation – it's not as sexy of course, but it's probably more authentic.

If you mean 'continuous improvement' when you've said 'innovative', then be clear. Define what you mean because if someone who's worked at Apple comes and works for your organization, they'll get very confused when you tell them they can't just change the world any time they want.

How do I get everyone to live the values?

I'm going to attempt to give you a short answer to this one. I could write a whole book on this question alone and I have spent half of my career helping people understand how to do this. Essentially you need to embed the values into everything you do and make them obvious. This is why it's essential to pick words that suit your business specifically. Here are a few suggestions that may work for your business:

- Make values fundamental to your recruitment process, and don't hire if the person can't prove they display them consistently, even if they are a technical superstar.
- Fire people based on your values. Yes this is ok. Behavior is 50% of performance.
- Regularly reward behavior that is consistent with the values.
- Teach people about the values and what you expect to see.
- Pick (or don't pick) your suppliers based on your values. This is a tough one. A client had 'Safety above all else' as one of their values. "Do you always live this?" I asked. "Of course" was

the reply. "Even when two contracts are presented and one is cheaper but they don't have the same safety record?" I followed up. "Ummm…"

- Allow people time to understand what the values mean for them in their work.
- Have regular conversations about the values and how they are displayed in day-to-day work.
- Have a tool kit for managers which helps them to ask the right questions and give the right answers to their people.
- Ask your customers if you live your values. Scary I know, but damn powerful.

There are many other things that businesses do to implement and have fun with the values, like clever marketing slogans and equally clever 'employee of the month' awards, however your question was how to get your people to 'live' the values.

Key foundation stone 3 – Strategy

A strategy quite simply is the goals, objectives and activity that the business engages in to deliver on the vision. The way I like to think about is this that the vision/mission is the destination, and the strategy is the map that tells you how to get to the destination. It's important that the strategy is very clear and directly aligned to the delivery of the vision. A strategy isn't all things to all people. A strategy doesn't contain the day-to-day activities of a business.

For example, a strategy won't contain payroll or accounts receivable. They are day-to-day activities that must happen to keep the business functional so there is no need to place them in the strategy.

A great strategy keeps it simple. It's clear about the company objectives, the high-level activity and the measurements. It has a direct alignment to the delivery and achievement of the vision. Great strategy is essential for delivering the kind of results that businesses want.

A great strategy will also contain a guide to how the business will FORM, FLOW and FEEL. The objectives in the strategy will ensure that the vision and the values are realized. This is how the strategy and culture are intertwined, rather than at odds.

Culture eats strategy for breakfast.

This statement has been attributed to author and thought leader Peter Drucker. Whether Drucker said it this way or not (there doesn't appear to be a true citation for the quote), the sentiment has stuck and is repeated regularly by business leaders everywhere.

Culture eats strategy for breakfast. But does it really?

It appears that this colloquial phrase is trying to demonstrate the importance culture plays in the delivery of results. If your culture is not facilitating the outcome of your business strategy, then the strategy becomes useless.

The danger with this statement is businesses pitting the strategy and culture against each other. Culture is eating strategy, so there must be a clear winner. This is a destructive way of viewing culture.

Let's change this statement to "Culture and strategy go out for breakfast."

Culture and strategy are intrinsically linked. Strategy is what you do and culture is how you do it. It's not one or the other, it must be both.

You need a clear, understandable and relevant strategy that tells people the direction you are heading. If this remains in your head, or worse you don't know the direction you are heading, then you will never establish a culture that creates the kind of success you desire. People need to be able to see the direction they are heading because they want to know that the time and energy that they are giving your business is worthwhile. A basic need for all humans is to feel that they are contributing and even better than that, they are contributing to something meaningful. A strategy allows this to occur.

Just get on with it and write the strategy down. You can write it anyway you want, however, if you want to be certain that your people are clear about what you are doing, then have the following elements in your strategy:

- The overarching goal/purpose (i.e. Why you are doing what you are doing – this is generally an explanation of the end game and what key objectives are going to help you reach your vision)
- What you are going to do to achieve results/objectives, including:
  - Living the corporate values (i.e. how you behave makes all the difference to success)

- o The priorities for running the business (these are things like customer experience, return on investment, and workforce – i.e. how you achieve results)
- o The priorities for your customers (these are things like the products you are producing, and the services that you provide – i.e. what results you are achieving)
- How you will measure success (i.e. timeframes, key performance indicators, and targets)

You can add other elements to your strategy if you feel the need, however these are the essential elements that will guide the success of your business and provide you with a basis for your structures.

Other foundation stones

Other foundation stones are leadership, customer and structures (including governance).

In Chapter 4 we explored the role of the leader in culture change. Leading, **leadership**, being a leader…. clearly this topic can be explored further, thousands of books have been written on the subject, millions of hours of training have been devoted to it. I'm not going to speak on the role of the leader here other than to say – investing in your leaders will give you your biggest bang for your buck in culture transformation. Without strong leadership vision, values and capabilities, your program will crumble. Without having a clear and documented understanding of the expectations you have of your leaders, your program will falter. The role of the leader is so significant that I've already started another book based on my research and many interactions with leaders over the last 20 years. It will describe in detail how the leader influences the culture, so stay tuned for that one.

Frequently when people hear the term '**structure**' it worries them – or at least it makes them sigh, a long fateful sigh. Often a new CEO or a manager comes into the business and their first action is to restructure the team in a way that makes sense to them. This happens time and time again and, depending on how good the organization is at responding to change, it can take a lot of energy and time, and may erode the trust that the people within the business have with the management of the business. The fear for many people is that they will lose their job and be out of work. Structure change gets a bad rap because of how often the change process is screwed up – I think some managers forget that there are people attached to the boxes on the Visio chart they are playing with.

Creating an appropriate structure in the business is important, because structures help the work flow through the business. They help with maintaining accountability and they help with ensuring that people feel safe and secure in the organization in which they work. There are multitudes of different types of structure and organizational design of structure. You'll find countless books written about organizational structure design, many of them are useful and many are not. There are a few principles of good organizational design that allow you to put structures into place that facilitate good work flow.

The principles of a good organizational design are as follows:

1. Let go of the way it has been done before, you are changing for a reason. Don't allow yourself to just shift boxes around on an organizational chart. Really look at what is needed for your business.
2. Allow your top talent to help you to create the best structure for the work and the best use of their skills.
3. Develop the organizational structure chart last, the lines and boxes will become clear once you determine what you are trying to achieve.
4. Understand the skills/capabilities/tasks to get the outcomes required to who you group together to be most effective.

5. Determining an effective, non-bureaucratic, accountability structure (i.e. who is responsible for the performance of others).
6. Clarify how decisions are made, who has authority to make decisions, and how far up the chain does a decision need to go before its made... hint: the closer decisions are to the work outcome the better.
7. What work is best to be centralised and what is best decentralised (e.g. who is responsible for developing business plans, workforce plans, and budgets – a central team of experts, or the managers, or perhaps a mix of both).

A good place to start with organizational design is to review the strategy and the businesses key systems of work (SOW). The SOW will allow you to review the success of the work flow through the business. Are there gaps, are there redundant processes, is there a bottle-neck?

The next step is to review the skills, capabilities and tasks required to deliver on the strategy and vision. You can then assess where the skill gaps are. If you can fill the skill gaps by moving your people into other positions and retraining, then that is a good situation to be in. If you don't have the skills required, or the skills that are available are no longer required, then you are in recruitment and redundancy territory – if you aren't skilled in these two Rs then engage a capable Human Resource professional to assist you.

I'm not going to underestimate the amount of fear that these processes cause, and I'm not going to underestimate the need in many businesses to change the structure and remove positions, and people, that are no longer productive. I don't advocate using restructure as a method of performance management. This process should occur regardless of the structure of the business. However, I won't shy away from the reality that many businesses have allowed productivity and capability to slip. This means that there are people in the business that are not going to contribute to your ongoing success and its time that they leave. If you have the capacity to pay a redundancy then all the better to make change. It allows people to leave with dignity. Rather than being fired, they can tell people about the redundancy opportunity they were provided. Sometimes restructure is the best outcome for unproductive people and gives them the much needed, kick in the rear, that they sometimes need for positive change.

Overall, the vision, the values, the strategy, leadership and the structure of your business should assist you to create business outcomes that you desire.

Key Take-away

If vision is the destination, then culture and strategy are how you get there.

Self-coaching Questions

- How could our business vision be more inspiring for our people?
- How can we explore what our customers think of us?
- How can our strategy contribute to our success?
- What capabilities and behaviors are needed so the business can deliver our vision?

Chapter 8:
FLOW – Start with the End in Mind

> *"We need to understand that failure is not the opposite of success, it's part of success."*
>
> Arianna Huffington, Founder
> Huffington Post

"You have to be purposeful when creating your culture. It must deliver the results you want and this won't happen by accident." – Michelle T Holland

Chapter 8: FLOW – Start with the End in Mind

A few years ago I was helping a local government organization that had been trying to change their culture for years. They couldn't understand why their staff surveys kept telling them that they didn't have a high tolerance for risk and why the scores on the culture survey weren't changing. The organization had prided itself on the significant innovation that had been executed in their community. When I joined their journey I spoke to the people within the business. From what they told me it was clear that this innovation happened *despite* the practices of the business, not because of them. This became evident when they tried to replicate this innovative practice in other areas of the business. The Executive finally acknowledged that although the project was innovative, it was deployed because of the sheer tenacity of three key project team members, not because the business was set up for innovation.

As we dug deeper and looked at other processes and practices they realized that the innovation wouldn't have occurred if the project team followed the company rules. The rules around managing people, finances and risk were restrictive and delayed change for months.

Let me highlight an example – their recruitment process was hierarchy-determined, without the agility required for innovation. When a position became vacant, the manager of the position would determine whether or not to recruit a position. However, before they could finalize that decision, they were required to speak to the HR department. From there, the HR department would then sign off with the manager, and the manager will take it to their general manager, and the general manager would then review, ask all the same questions that the HR officer had asked, before they would sign off on the position.

At times, the general manager wouldn't have time to ask all these questions and would sign off on the position anyway. The position then would get loaded on to the recruitment site, whereby another HR person would review the position description and create an advertisement which had to go through the same sign off process. At the end of the week, another HR person would print off all of the jobs and send them to the executive meeting for sign off by the general managers and the CEO. Once that it occurred, the position could be launched on the recruitment site. The interview would occur and a candidate would be selected. This process, when it was efficient, took a minimum of four weeks...

Prior to that candidate being given an offer of employment, the process had another round of sign offs, including the CEO. The candidate would finally receive an offer of employment, sometimes two or three months after they started the process... Can you imagine a candidate with an innovation mindset hanging around that long?

I'm hoping that in describing this very common process that you can clearly see the structure and the practice of this process was not congruent with how they wanted to be known.

There's a saying that I use in these situations... "The audio and the video are out of sync." Meaning that the business is saying 'we're innovative', but when you view what they are doing, they're anything but.

To create a great business your practices must be congruent with your goals… i.e. your audio and video must be in sync. To assess if you are in sync, ask yourself the following:

Are your processes, policies, procedures and systems facilitating people to get great results for the customer… or do they get in the way and hold people back from success?

It's easy to say, oh yes, our systems are reviewed regularly and they are best practice. However, when you ask your people what frustrates them the most out of everything, the one thing that comes up over and over is 'red tape'. The second is 'We don't have consistent processes'. This question can't be answered in a sweeping yes or no. This is where the real work of culture transformation occurs. This is where you need to roll up your sleeves and get down and dirty with the change. You need to analyze each of your systems and procedures to find out if they are facilitating or debilitating your business outcomes.

Culture is systemic and will only be transformed when the work your business is responsible for flows through your business in a systematic and streamlined way. Your processes, practices, systems and policies are the support structures that will hold your culture exactly where it is, therefore they must be a critical focus point for your culture change efforts. Yep, recreating a process is not as fun as attending a training workshop, but it will have more impact in the long term.

The FLOW part of the puzzle

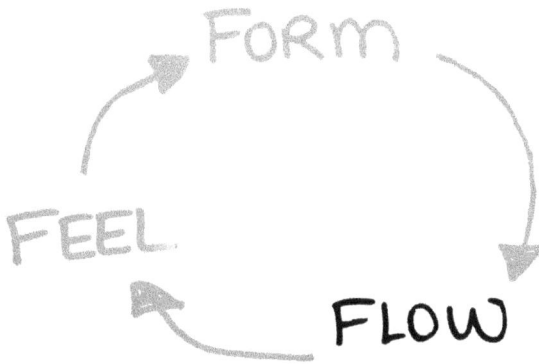

Examine if the work is flowing easily through your business and review the following:

- Information, Data and Knowledge – management, sharing, leveraging
- Planning systems – business, budget, organization performance, goals
- Decision making – empowerment, delegation, autonomy
- Capabilities and Behaviors – values alignment, interaction with people and systems
- Leadership and Management practice – leading people, managing results
- Process, Policies and systems – automated, effective, user focused, documented
- Development systems – growth, current, stretch goals
- Communication systems – information flow, consultation, access
- People systems – recruit, retain, reward and redirect
- Performance systems – role clarity, structure, accountability, alignment

The above elements are the work systems and structures that we put into business to keep the culture 'exactly' where it is. Therefore if you want to transform your business you need to change the structural elements that hold the ineffective practices in place.

When you examine this element of the model it becomes crystal clear why most culture transformation programs do not work. The majority of programs are focused on only one or two areas of culture. Businesses generally try to tackle the behavior and leadership competencies by putting on training programs. This is because it's seen as the simplest and most effective way to get change. Sadly this is only the beginning and too many business leaders fail to get the results they need. You must use an integrated model of planning for change, which also includes making tough decisions and managing the tough stuff.

Managing the tough stuff

In a recent episode of *Freakonomics*, my favorite podcast, they were discussing the gender pay gap. The interviewer spoke to a group of economists working with Uber. They determined that Uber was a closed economy which was not subject to discrimination. They hypothesized that there would not be a gender pay gap and therefore be able to once and for all name discrimination as the key to this gap. Surprisingly they found that Uber drivers still had a 7% gender pay gap, i.e. women earnt 7% less than men per hour doing the same work. What they determined was three causes for the gap. One, was the choices men and women made around the timing of fares – i.e. men were more likely to work the night shift. Two, men worked more hours so their experience with what fares to pick up and which ones to drop ensured they got the best fares. Three, men drove faster and thus were able to pick up more fares per hour. The last one accounted for 50% of the gap.

What does this have to do with culture? Well, number one and three are choices made by men and women because of society pressures. Women are less likely to drive in perceived unsafe conditions, such as at night. Given that one in four women report to being a survivor of assault (stats from National Sexual Violence Resource Centre), is it any surprise they aren't driving more at night? Men are more likely to speed. There is a perception in society that men are real men if they take risks. Heaven forbid that they are called a pussy or a nerd for driving slowly.

This outcome from the gender pay gap study at Uber shows the impact that society's culture has on outcomes. You are aware of the lack of women at CEO and Board Level. When you think about the structures we place around these things, e.g. board meetings happening in the evening, coupled with the fact that women are still twice as likely to do home duties as their male partners (stats from OECD), is it any wonder that women aren't on boards more? Of course this is huge subject, without a simple answer. However, I'm using it to highlight the importance of structural elements in culture change. If, for example, all board meetings were moved to 9:30 am instead of 6 pm… maybe more women could attend and be part of the board. But does this simple change happen? No, because it wouldn't suit the others on the board who are happy to meet after hours. What if this simple change is the compromise needed to change the culture of women on boards?

Managing the tough stuff and making tough decisions are essential for culture transformation. Your culture won't happen without them. It's great to put on a feel good training program or award's night. These things make your people feel like they matter, so they are important, but they aren't the only solution to culture problems. If you don't also manage the poor performance, the inappropriate behaviors, indirect behaviors, and the ineffective systems, your culture training will lose its value and people will become more cynical about the change process than they already were.

Processes and Culture

As far as culture is concerned, there must be an expectation that processes are kept as simple as possible, if not simpler. Processes are needed to run a successful business, but when the process becomes the focus of someone's job instead of facilitating the outcome… you're in trouble. I've worked with big government agencies, who have teams of people employed to manage processes because they are so complex. Does that sound efficient to you?

A question that you can ask yourself when developing a process is "Does this process add value to the outcome that the business is delivering for the customer?"

When I say customer, I'm talking about the ultimate customer. The ultimate customer is the person that will be utilizing the service or buying the product. Does the process that you're developing add value to that product? Does it add value to the service? Would the customer experience a greater benefit from the outcome because of this process? Would your customer be ok to pay for that procedure as part of their purchase price… because they are now…

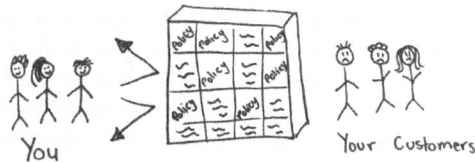

Your processes may be what is standing in the way of a great customer experience.

Don't kid yourself that having outdated procedures or cumbersome policies don't add to your bottom line, they do. Too often I speak with managers about their team's culture and they tell me that the culture would be better if they just had more people to do the work. The people are just overworked. Your people are so busy trying to climb the great wall of policies and procedures they don't have time to serve the customer.

Several years ago I was hired as a HR Manager and had a team of four people. The business wasn't large and therefore the number of people appeared suitable. However, when I started, the team told me how overworked and burnt out they were and that they needed another HR Administrator to help with the burden. I was new to the business so I could have just believed this assessment and hired an extra person. However, instead, I reviewed the work that they were doing and discovered that the current administration officer was spending 45% of her time doing low value work and another 10% working to maintain outdated systems. This inefficiency was consistent across the team.

Instead of a new person to manage the systems, I hired a temporary project officer to redesign the systems. When the project was complete my team gained back 10–20% productivity which allowed them to commence work that added additional value to the business and was meaningful. The administration officer regained 40% of her time by removing non-value work from her day. This meant that the role could be utilized more efficiently and I didn't have to hire another officer.

Of course as a manager you are busy too, so the easy way is to just hire someone else and hope for the best. Sadly, that rarely works. When changing culture, there is no easy way out. The easy ways put more pressure on the already inefficient culture and processes.

This means that you must think laterally about the processes in your care and think seriously about what kind of value they add. In most organizations there are processes and systems that impede good customer service. This is because over time, people have implemented a process to make *their* life easier, rather than add *value* to the customer. If you look at any of the process improvement management models – like Six Sigma or Lean etc. – they will insist that you make your processes as simple as possible so that they add value to the outcome of the customers' receiving.

Unfortunately, the baseline principles of these models get thrown away because people are designing processes that are making their life easier. It is human nature to want simplicity for yourself, but a process should never be designed for the operator without strict adherence to understanding the impact on the customer. Those ten payroll forms that managers have to fill in to get a new employee paid may make payroll's life easier, but they are a burden for the manager. If ten managers are filling out ten forms and then payroll are processing them, that is 200 pieces of paper that are going through someone's hands. Oh and of course payroll double check everything, so it's actually 300… you have to ask yourself what this 'easy' process is costing your business. A conservative and quick calculation based on the average Australian wage for a manager and payroll officer, and assuming each form takes five minutes to complete/process, and you are only hiring ten people per year… that is approximately $4000 p.a. you are spending on that very simple process that no one is thinking about. Imagine how much you are spending on your budgeting, or reporting, or recruitment processes?

In large businesses, I have discovered positions which are easily redundant. However, the person within that position looks extraordinarily busy because they're constantly managing a process that they have developed. If I'm being a cynic, I could say that they've developed, or at least maintained, this process to keep themselves in the job. In large organizations, it would be interesting to do an analysis on how many positions have been created to manage processes. If I make a guess based on my experience, I'd guess between 10–15% of positions within a business are not necessary if you remove or redesign the process. Therefore the position would become redundant thus saving the business money in the long term, or enabling that resource to be allocated to more value adding work.

A couple of years ago I worked with a not-for-profit organization doing extraordinarily valuable work in the community. At that time they had approximately one hundred staff. Twenty-five of these people were in low-level administration roles. The administration roles included data entry, reception and general administration. Twenty-five administration roles for an organization of 100 people. This is astounding and, unless the business model is in selling administration services, then having 25% of your workforce as administration means that your processes and your systems are creating work for your people. They're not helpful in delivering outcomes for your customers.

I'm going to be controversial here so hold on to your hats governance and structure lovers…

Great workplaces are *not* built on the back of policy and procedures. If anything they get in the way of having a great culture and awesome performance. Policy and procedure are the easy way out… great leaders and managers flourish when they aren't tied up in 'the rules'.

Having an 'Attraction' policy won't attract great people.

Having a 'Retention' policy won't keep great people.

Having a 'Performance' policy won't ensure top performance.

Having an 'Ethics' policy won't stop someone stealing from you.

Having a 'Rewards and Recognition' policy won't give you happy staff.

Policy and procedures are useful when done right because they give you a consistent standard. Having too many policies in place can create a reliance on being told how to behave, how to work and how to manage. Why think for yourself when there's a policy for everything? Are your policies creating a lazy management approach?

"But I did exactly what the retention policy said and my staff member still left. So obviously, it's not my fault." Said the Unaccountable Manager

Now I'm not saying you shouldn't have systems to help you run your business, on the contrary, systems are essential… but they are not the end… they are just the beginning.

After years of working with many great organizations, and many bad ones, I've noticed a trend. Policies and procedures are not helping leaders to lead. And they rarely help managers to manage.

I'm sure that you're not shocked by this trend, nor would it shock you if I told you that many leaders and team members persist with inefficient processes. If you want to have a great business then you will need to think about it differently, and do things differently. Here's a few ideas for you to consider instead of implementing a new round of written policies:

Don't be a jerk: treat your people well, treat your colleagues well, treat your customers well. Contrary to the Hollywood depiction, you don't have to be a jerk to be a boss.

Communicate honestly and often: don't be afraid of the truth or giving/receiving feedback. The truth is only bad when you forget that last piece of advice (i.e. don't be a jerk).

Have skilled leaders at all levels: having leadership capabilities and skills embedded across the business increases the expectations of good leadership in everyone.

Have skilled managers at all levels: managers are not leaders and leaders are not managers. Financials, projects, objectives, and otherwise. Stuff and things need to be managed, people need to be led.

Set clear expectations and manage performance: you have no right to hold people accountable for expectations not set. Set the performance expectations and then hold them accountable.

Continual learning, changing, flexing and growing: workplaces are not a 'set and forget' activity. As the leader you must look for ways of innovating not only your products and service but also your workplace. Also, provide an environment whereby your people can do the same.

Keep it simple: if you must have written policies then keep them simple and focused on the principles above, and the accountabilities and outcomes you want to achieve.

Employ and grow skilled people that actually want to create a great business and skilled leaders that can guide others towards great outcomes.

Policies and procedures don't create great businesses, people do.

Process and System Review
The reality is that many businesses have a lot of processes in place and many of them are not adding value. Therefore you must undertake

a process review and redesign them, or remove them to enable your business to become one that is profitable and that people love.

The most important part of understanding and reviewing the flow of the business is to ensure that everything you do adds value and doesn't stand in the way of great customer outcomes. If a system causes a delay to customer service then it must be redesigned or removed. You can't be afraid to completely remove a process. If you allow the fear of making someone's job redundant, or breathing in the fire of the risk manager, then you'll never make the change you need. A good rule of thumb is to get the people you think are going to be opposed to the change involved at the beginning.

Below are six principles of process and system review that you can use when developing systems and a framework of systems. I've also provided suggestions about where to start looking. In my experience these systems aren't as efficient as they should be. They also affect many people in the business. Keep it simple is my philosophy. Your principles of change don't need to be overly complicated.

Let's call this the 'best bang for your buck' process review guide:

Principles of good system review:	Where to start:
• Less is more – only have processes that add to the customer experience, reduce/remove others • Keep it simple – make everything as simple as possible, then go simpler • Value – understand what each system costs you in time, money, reputation etc. • Alignment – bring like processes together (e.g. business, workforce, and budget planning) • Perfection is a killer – they don't have to be perfect, just functional • Get people involved – the people using the systems will know the pain points • Legislation – abide by legislation, but don't be scared of it.	• Customer – start with the direct customer-facing process • Human resources – performance management, recruitment and induction • Governance – policy frameworks, record keeping • Financial management – budgeting, purchasing, procurement, credit cards. • Performance Reporting – financial, KPIs, decision making processes • Technology – use IT to get rid of redundant and low value work, don't over complicate it though – some systems are harder to use than they are worth.

You'll notice that the principles I've listed here are not brain science or rocket surgery… yes I just said that. It is just simple practical advice to get you started immediately. Taking strict care of the way in which the work flows through your business is essential to creating a profitable and enjoyable business. If you skip this bit or hold on too tightly to your processes you are setting your business up for failure. Don't allow the scary legislation cheerleaders stop you from creating a functional business. Yes, risk mitigation and safety are important, but question whether all the forms are necessary.

Local processes and departmental work

Many of the systems I've listed above are the central systems that keep a business functioning. However, they are not the only business systems that add inefficiencies to the business. Local processes that are created by teams to help them often become cumbersome and boring. Take non-technical/project meetings that people are required to attend. For example committee meetings, quarterly performance reviews or team meetings.

Do your people lament about having to go to these meetings?
If yes, then your meetings are not working for you or your culture and need to change.

Meetings can be used to increase culture but too often I see them destroying it.

Generally the complaints I hear about meetings are:
- They go for too long
- There are too many of them
- They don't achieve anything
- They are a waste of time
- They are boring

Sadly, face to face meetings have gotten the raw end of the deal. They can drive business culture when done well. When they are receiving the above reviews then it's fair to say you have some work to do.

Here are a few simple tips to create meetings that add value:

1. Set clear and succinct outcome focused agendas – don't include items that can be managed elsewhere or have been discussed elsewhere. Your agenda doesn't have to be written in a special template, just jot it on the whiteboard.

2. Be clear about your expectations for each member – people at the meeting will engage more if they are clear about what is expected of them. Pop your expectation in the meeting invite so they can come prepared.

3. Only have people at the meeting who need to be there – if you are doing updates then have one person per team there and set an expectation that they will share information. If you hear that information is not being shared, hold them accountable.

4. Ensure the chair has the skills to chair the meeting – stick to task and the agenda. If you go off-topic the chair should be assessing if the topic adds value to the meeting or not and is able to bring people back to task.

5. There must be no passengers in meetings – if you have a quiet person/s in the meeting that never adds value, question why they are in the meeting. If they must be there, discuss with them what they are expected to do in the meeting. Note – be mindful of reflective thinkers and ensure that the chair is allowing time for them to think and speak and asking for their input.

6. Team meetings are good for getting people together, but there are better ways. Look for better ways to share time and information with your team members. Standing check-ins are good for information sharing because people stay succinct when they are not lounging in a chair.

Essentially create meetings that are valuable and outcomes focused. When people are clear about what is expected they are more likely to be involved.

And… cut your meetings by half… I bet there are other ways you can achieve the result you want… so be creative and find them.

The flow of the business needs to be effective and efficient.

You have to be really practical during this stage of culture review so that your business functions effectively. Be prepared that this will take time, effort, energy, work and frustrations. You can't transform a business in five minutes.

You must have a vision and a future direction that you're working towards. You must have effective systems that get the outcomes you desire. You must have appropriately skilled leaders to take you and your people there.

Once the business is formed (i.e. vision, values, leadership etc.) and the flow of the work (i.e. processes, systems, technology, communication) is sorted out, then you can get on with the task of creating a business that people love. This is what's going to take your business to a whole other level.

Culture is the way the business forms, flows and feels.

Let's talk about how people feel about your business.

Key Take-away

The flow of the business includes all systems, process and practices and if your systems aren't reviewed for effectiveness, you are missing a critical step in creating a business that is profitable and that people love.

Self-coaching Questions

- How can our systems of work be more effective?
- What do past reviews or feedback say about the systems and processes we're responsible for?
- How can we add more value to our customer while reducing costs?
- How can we reduce the frustration our people and our customers feel about our business systems?

Chapter 9:
FEEL –
Start with You

> *"I don't go by the rule book. I lead from the heart, not the head."*

Diana, Princess of Wales

"When you genuinely care for your people, they will genuinely care for your customers."
– Michelle T Holland

Chapter 9: FEEL – Start with You

"Is your heart really in this?"

This is a question that people drag out when they're talking to a team member who appears to be disengaged. People often use the term 'heart' to describe work.

"Is your heart in it?", "Are we getting to the heart of the matter?", "Have we captured the hearts and minds of our people?", "Put the customer at the heart of our decisions."

When people talk about being connected to a business, they talk about values being aligned. When they enjoy their job, they tell you that they love their work, they love the company that they work, they love the people they work with. When a customer talks about a coffee shop they go to, or the latest Apple product, they tell you emphatically how much they love it. 'Love' or other emotive words, roll off the tongue easily when people are settled within themselves, and truly enjoy the work they do and/or the teams that they're working with.

Why do we use these highly emotional terms to describe work?

Let's take a step back for a moment. Why do we work? Some people's immediate response is to get money to pay for my life. And they're absolutely, 100% correct. That is one of the reasons why we work. It's definitely one of the reasons I work. But it's not the only reason, or even the main one.

The other reason is actually much more important. There is a basic human need to contribute to society. There's a basic human desire to feel valued for that contribution. This is why values alignment is important to us when we're looking for a new job, or when we're leaving a job that hasn't worked for us. We say to our friends, "I'm resigning. I'm leaving the business." And when our friends ask us why, we tell them all of the events that have broken our trust with the business.

We use terms like "I love my job" or "I hate my job."

When we go for an interview and the interviewer says to us, "Why are you leaving that organization?", many people, particularly the ones who have been coached in good interview techniques, will say a version of 'our values don't align'.

We talk about this heart and emotion stuff all the time when we're talking about work. The sense of value is important for every human being… even for those hard-edged people who don't think it's important to them.

This is what this chapter is all about. It's about that connection to heart, purpose, and meaning. It's that connection that makes such a difference in organizations. How that connection is developed, and when it breaks, is important for your transformation journey.

Businesses who take the FORM and FLOW part of the culture puzzle seriously are generally the companies that have the employees who tell you how awesome it is to work there. How valued they feel. And of course, the opposite is true.

Remember, culture is the way a business forms, flows and feels…

The FEEL part of the puzzle is generally the element of this equation that people talk about the most when describing culture. The FEEL part is the reason that culture 'programs' are started in the HR department. But this is the biggest trap with culture. The FEEL occurs as a result of the first two elements, and therefore you need to take it damn seriously when you notice you have a problem in these areas. When you have a problem that you can FEEL, it's time for a reality check into the kind of business you are running.

Depending on how much is being felt by you or your employees determines the action you need to take. Many businesses just need a few tweaks in the flow area of the business to bring them back on track. Perhaps some coaching for their leaders to reconnect their hearts and minds with the business. But if you are 'feeling' obvious and negative effects of a broken culture, then it's time for a revolution, business transformation, or radical solution to get your business back on track.

FEEL, once established becomes part of the support structures that hold the culture in place.

The FEEL Part of the Puzzle

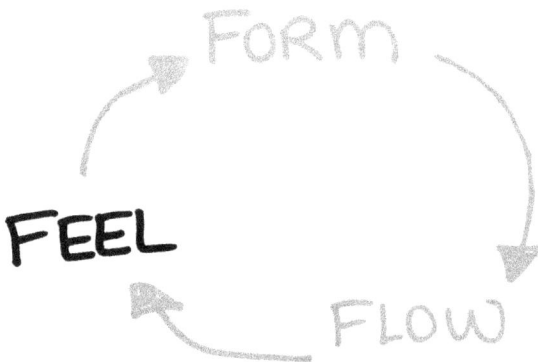

To truly understand the impact the form and flow elements are having on your business you must examine the following elements:

- Relationships – trust, collaboration, interdependence
- Motivation – engagement, intrinsic, extrinsic, personal preferences
- Enjoyment – people, work, engagement, feeling valued, stress
- Meaning – perceived significance and value of work contribution
- Alignment – vision and values (through goals and behavior)
- Social justice – respect, fairness, equity, compassion
- Customer loyalty – brand recognition, raving fans
- Results – quality, performance, profit, customers, people, communicating and celebrating results
- Agility – adaption, innovation, change

Generally, the root cause to problems in the FEEL list comes from the FORM and FLOW elements. When you notice the FEEL indicators are showing distress, it's time to address the issues you have with your FORM and FLOW areas of the business. Work through the past two chapters to help you identify the ones to work on. The result you are trying to achieve should give you a clue, or working with someone skilled in analysis will add value.

You must remember that although the FEEL of the business is the outcome of FORM and FLOW, the FEEL once embedded will guide the FORM and FLOW. It's a vicious cycle once you are in it.

For example, let's say quality results are the issue, start by reviewing your systems of work in the production area. Is there enough critical thinking? Are you purchasing quality ingredients? Are your people skilled? Is your budget appropriate?

But what if the people in your business are disengaged, or lack motivation, or they don't believe the work is meaningful? They are not going to give you the best results. Unless you can shift the thinking of these people, you may receive a change that is still ineffective and hasn't fixed the problem.

I'll address how to fix this cycle issue in Chapter 10 – 'Transforming Your Business'.

If you find that you still have a culture issue *AFTER* fixing the FORM and FLOW of the business, then you probably have a trust issue. This takes a lot more time to change... it won't happen overnight, but it will happen. By addressing your culture in a deliberate, thoughtful, and practical way, you will begin to improve the FEEL elements, including trust.

To address issues of trust there are three key things that you must focus on – you, your purpose, and your relationships.

As I mentioned earlier, Simon Sinek, talks extensively about the heart base connection people make with businesses, otherwise known as 'purpose' or 'the why'. He says "Start with why" because purpose is so important. I agree with him and believe purpose is essential, but I'm going to tell you to "Start with you" first. When you start with you, as the leader, it will help you to engage your people, who in turn will engage your customers.

The following image represents the way in which the work flows through a business. Unfortunately I hear business leaders talking about the customer and forgetting about themselves, and their people. They have a misunderstood belief that the people serve the business. They don't. They serve the customer, the leader serves the people, and the systems serve the leader... most businesses have this ass-about.

Who's serving who in your organisation?

Systems → Leader → Team → Customer

Let's start with you

How often as a leader do you put your needs first? If you pride yourself as a great leader, I'll bet, not often. It's your professional development that suffers. It's your paper that gets left to the last minute. It's your kids that don't get picked up from school. The problem with this is that as leaders we end up depleted with nothing to give. You need to make sure that you take care of your own needs so that you are able to take care of other's needs. This is why I'm asking you to spend time on you for a moment. However, this is not permission to send yourself to conferences, give yourself a pay rise and ignore your obligations to others… you're not a politician.

Starting with what makes you tick and what's important for you is essential to help you prioritize what is most important.

You could get a salary from anywhere or from any organization. You could start your own business (or another business), or freelance and earn money. You could play the share market and never have a 'real' job. Money is an outcome of the job that you do. It's not the motivation.

Once you understand YOU, it's going to be easy to connect yourself to a bigger purpose and a bigger why, which ultimately makes you a better leader and a better person. When you understand who YOU are and what your purpose is, it allows you to connect with people on a deeper level. When you are a business leader about to embark on change I believe that focusing on you is the most important thing you can do for your people, your customer, and your business.

One of the biggest mistakes that business leaders make is to focus all of their attention on trying to 'fix' their business model or their employees. The leaders who focus on knowing and growing themselves always have better long-term outcomes.

In the chapter on culture archetypes, you may have recognized yourself in one or two of the roles. This is a great way of digging into who you are, particularly when you are embarking on culture change journey. As a business leader, understanding yourself will help you understand the impact you are having on your people and business. Look at the impact that the culture archetypes have on your business and times it by three if you are a leader, perhaps times it by ten if you are the CEO or founder.

Prior to starting my own business, I worked mostly for organizations which were service-based. I connected to their mission and their vision because leaving the world in a better place than I found it is important for me.

Knowing this about myself allowed me to make conscious decisions about the kinds of employers I'd choose. Now that I run my own business I'm able to determine the kinds of clients that I help and enjoy working with.

I know that I'm a Dreamer/Imagineer. Knowing this about myself helps me to explain to new clients how I will work with them and what they can expect from me. My clients are clear that when we work together, I won't be writing long-winded recommendation papers that have no substance. They know that when they are with me I will fire questions at them like I'm an automatic machine gun from one of those old war movies. They are well aware that I will challenge them to be better and do better and that I'll come up with some ripper ideas that appear crazy at first look. If I didn't know who I was I would end up working with people who thought I'd just come in and run a little training program and get on with what they tell me to do. That's not me, and I don't work in that way. My clients are clear about what they will get from me, because I'm clear about who I am.

As a leader, I don't expect you to be perfect, but I do expect you to be constantly learning, growing and improving so that you can help your people and your business to grow and prosper.

"When we are no longer able to change a situation, we are challenged to change ourselves." – Viktor E Frankl

To find your purpose, look to the future.

If you want to discover more about you and your purpose, take your business to the next level and be an engaging and inspiring leader, then you must have a clear vision of your future. Not your next career move, nor your strategic business plan. I mean you need to look at the future that you want to live within, personally.

Looking at your personal future and having a clear vision is the most powerful exercise for business growth and change that I can recommend. The following activity is something that I recommend to every client I work with, and every friend who is seeking something more. Having a clear vision of how you want to live your life guides you in every decision you make.

Let's say you're a business leader, you might be the CEO, or the founder. I'm guessing that you at least have a team of people you are responsible for, otherwise you'd be reading *Harry Potter* instead of a book about business transformation. The scenario that I want you to start with is *your* ideal future. Not someone else's vision of your future. This is not an interview question. This is about being truthful with yourself and what you actually want from life – if you don't know the answer to this you'll continue to make poor choices, at work and at home. I know it feels uncomfortable to focus on you, and you'd prefer that I give you a step by step process to use to 'fix' your employees motivation or engagement problems. Just trust me on this and give it a go, ok?

What Does Your Future Look Like?

Don't take yourself just two or three years into the future. What I actually want you to do is take yourself ten years into the future. If you want a successful, creative, engaging business where your employees and your customers are absolutely lining up at your door – what does that look like? If you are a team manager, think about it from the context of your team and the service that you provide.

Having a clear vision keeps you and your team motivated.

Let's assume that you're going to be in this business for another ten years, because it is the ideal business and why would you leave if you're having an ideal experience? The technique is to write down that ideal experience and write it down in some significant detail. Pick a day in the life of you as a business leader ten years into the future.

What are you experiencing? What are your people saying about your business? What feedback are you getting from your customers? What is happening that's making you really proud? What are you doing? How are people talking to each other? What are your customers/the media saying about you? What does your bottom line look like?

Even explore what you are doing, at work and at home. Is work supporting your life? Where did you wake up? Do you have the flexibility to take your dog for a long walk in the morning? Can you pick your kids up from school or spend time with them in school holidays? Are you having two or three holidays a year? Are you golfing on a Friday?

Think big, because it's your future so you may as well enjoy it. Plus if your outside of work future is not being supported by your inside of work future, then something is going to give.

After truly exploring your ideal day, stay in the future and ask...

When I look back over the last ten years, what are the changes that I have made to get here?

This is really a good way of being able to explore, not only your vision and your why for your business, but also what you need to do to get there. A goal remains a dream if you don't take deliberate action.

This action will help you to understand your true purpose. Your purpose is not to get up, go to work, pay bills and die... there is so much more to life.

Now... relationships

The final thing that I want to explore with you is relationships. Relationships are essential for getting the best out of your people and the best for your customer. If you think about it simplistically, your customer will continue to come back to you if they are having a great experience. And the way in which they are going to have a great experience is not through you, the business owner or the business leader, it is actually through the people who are serving your customer. Your role as a leader is to take care of those people and ensure that their experience is such that they can create a memorable, high-quality experience for your customer. You take care of your people and they will take care of your customers for you.

The best place to start to build your relationships with your people is through conversation, and genuine conversation to boot! How do you have a genuine conversation with someone and make it meaningful for them?

In Chapter 4 we explored what people want from a leader, including compassion, and I introduced you to my catch cry, just be human first. When you focus on the person and your relationship you will engage with them in a meaningful way and foster trust. Of course you will be talking to them about work, but you'll do it through a heart-to-heart conversation.

This will be the biggest challenge that I lay down for many people reading this book, particularly those of you that have come from the old school of thought that you leave your personal stuff at the door.

"Why can't they just leave their personal stuff at the door?" Sighed the exhausted manager.

The reality is that humans cannot do that. And try as we might, we are creatures that are driven by emotion. If your employee, teammate, or manager is struggling in their personal world, then it's going to be difficult for them to just put that aside and pretend that it's not happening. If you're asking your people to pretend that a part of their life does not exist, then you're missing an opportunity to connect with them and build trust.

I'm not saying that you reduce your performance expectations and become their best buddy. But you can be a practical leader who treats people with respect. If a team member is dealing with a significant challenge in their personal life, possibly their performance will drop. Are they a terrible person who needs to be fired? No, they are a person who needs compassion and support so that they can get back to performing in a way that they feel proud. More often than not, the person whose performance has dropped knows it and feels awful about it already.

If you come from a human place first and have focused on creating strong relationships through genuine conversations, you will be much more tolerant about minor and short-lived performance drops. You know the kind of person they are, you know what performance you normally get from them, and you know that they are going through some tough stuff.

Sheryl Sandberg, the Chief Operating Officer at Facebook, explored the impact of grief and loss in her book *Option B* which she co-wrote with psychologist Adam Grant. A heart-breaking and honest story that Sandberg tells in her book is her return to Facebook after the sudden death of her husband Dave. Sandberg wasn't prepared for his death, and like many people who lose the love of their life, her grief took over her abilities. She reflects on the pain that she felt not only for the loss of Dave but also for the loss of her abilities in the workplace. She felt terrible that her value to the business was compromised. Sandberg said that she had trouble focusing, rambled, and even fell asleep in an executive meeting. That night she called Facebook CEO Mark Zuckerberg to tell him, "Maybe it's too soon. I made a total fool of myself."

He replied with, "Lots of people sleep in meetings!" He then added, "But I think you made a really important point today," and noted what it was. He told her that she can choose to return whenever she was ready, but that he wanted to let her know that she helped the team even during her difficult first day back. He acknowledged her pain and struggle, while still pointing out where she contributed… nice one Markie Z.

Sadly we often overlook the impact of personal struggles on people and don't acknowledge that it will affect their performance in the short term. If we don't support them and recognize that they can get back to performance, they may question their value and their worth. By treating people within our workplaces the same as we would our friends and family, it will help them be much more engaged and pull out of performance slumps quickly.

This is just how we handle short-term performance issues, ie: issues that are out of character for the person. If you are dealing with long-term performance problems or capability gaps, then you need to have a different conversation and implement a different process. We should still expect performance over the longer term. If performance is still suffering after a sustained period (e.g. a couple of months), then a conversation needs to occur about how that performance can be improved and/or how the outcomes will happen with or without the person within that position.

This is handling serious matters of course. Being able to show compassion through these times is really important, but just being human first starts with the little day-to-day things. Building great relationships with your people, so that you build trust, takes effort. It starts with developing an interest in them. It starts with having conversations with them. It starts with asking them how their weekend was and genuinely caring about how their weekend was. It starts with talking to them about their performance, acknowledging the things that they do really well, reinforcing the activities that they engage in that are helpful, and it's about helping them learn and grow from situations that don't go well.

If you don't feel skilled in having a genuine conversation around performance, start developing your feedback muscle by giving easy feedback, i.e. congratulate them for a job well done.

Don't make the mistake that thousands of leaders make each year. They ignore the impact that they have on the culture and the people around them. They ignore the fact that what your people and your customers experience is the outcome of the culture you are creating.

When you are clear about who you are, why you do what you do, and what makes you tick, you and the people you work with are able to get the best out of you. If you don't spend the time truly understanding and investing in you and your leadership style, you are destined to fail slowly (which is the worst kind of failing).

But I know that you want a few ideas about how to change the FEEL of your business so here are a few things that I've done with other clients to assist them to add value to their culture program while they tackle the FORM and FLOW elements of the business:

1. Culture days – fun and educational days spent with the team. The focus is on the how of work and about learning a new skill aligned to the company values.

2. Behavior change workshops – active workshops with plenty of time to explore the individual's impact on culture.

3. Leadership and individual coaching – providing coaching to your managers and key people to assist them to build capabilities to manage and create change.

4. Team communication – keep communication open, honest and regular. Create new ways of communicating, eg: standing, walking or over lunch meetings.

5. Visual management – provide elements that are important to people, such as current performance indicators, priorities, responses to staff surveys, training events etc. When it's visual it's more interesting and gets used.

Be creative.

Key Take-away

Culture is systemic. When you address the root cause, i.e. the FORM and FLOW issues, your people and your customers will feel better about your business. Also remember that the culture you are changing is the culture you are working in… don't let it hold you back.

Self-coaching Questions

- How can you focus more attention on you?
- How can you fill your own cup so that you can fill others?
- How are you and your business responding to the way people feel?
- What processes could be removed or changed to reduce frustration and disengagement?
- How are you building and/or damaging trust?

Chapter 10:
Transform your Business

"The Golden Rule of Habit Change: You can't extinguish a bad habit, you can only change it."

Charles Duhigg

"The real work of culture transformation occurs when you roll up your sleeves and get down and dirty with the change." - Michelle T Holland

Chapter 10: Transform your Business

Let's get down to brass tacks.

It's all very well for you to know what culture is and what makes it up, but without a clear and actionable plan of attack it will stay exactly where it is now.

I'm hoping by now you understand why focusing on culture is essential for your business. And that you understand that culture isn't a touchy feely thing that the HR department worries about. Culture is yours. It is yours to make or to break, so let's get busy.

This is a very short chapter with a practical guide to planning for change. You will find graphics and information that show you how I plan. If you would like a template all you need to do is go to synergyiq.com.au and look under resources. It's available for free download.

Below is a step-by-step plan for culture transformation. If you need help with any of the steps please contact us at synergyiq.com.au and one of my team will happily speak with you about how we can help.

However, try it yourself first. You never know, you may just have a breakthrough.

Just remember that culture doesn't have an end date, its enduring, but your culture transformation effort should.

Here's the ideal situation which will help you deal with the issues talked about in the FLOW chapter, i.e. that vicious cycle you may find yourself in because the culture you are trying to change is the one you are living in. I have found the greatest success comes from the business investing the time, effort and resources in the transformation for a set period of time, and has the support of an expert to guide them along the way.

> *"If you think it's expensive to hire an expert, wait till you hire an amateur."* – Anonymous

Here are my recommendations for setting yourself up for success:
- Culture transformation is managed like a project with plans, milestones, budgets, resources, objectives and structure. However, because of the nature of culture change, an agile project management approach is more aligned. Although traditionally a software project approach, the principles of agile work beautifully with culture transformation.
- A team of experts are brought together to work on the transformation and support the rest of the business to create change. They can come from within the business as long as they have the capability and the support to grow and perform.
- The leadership team are skilled in leading transformation.
- The CEO is accountable for the success of the project, including setting clear expectations of the people and leaders, communication messages, maintaining momentum, and holding their people accountable for action.
- The project is managed by a business transformation expert, and deployed by people with facilitation, coaching and change leadership skills.

- There needs to be appropriate flexibility and agility within the project scope to respond to the culture change as it happens.
- The actions must be integrated and deployed in a way that ensures success (i.e. FORM, FLOW and FEEL).
- Behavior and culture training for people should happen in concert with the above actions to enable a seamless change and skill people to deliver change.

Plan for success

Let's talk about the plan. I've provided you with the ideal state, and now I'm going to tell you how to plan for change. Leaders can feel overwhelmed with the amount of change required and wonder where to start.

At the beginning of course…

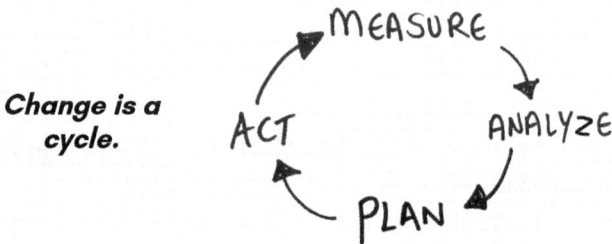

Change is a cycle. ACT → MEASURE → ANALYZE → PLAN →

Step 1: Future State

Without understanding where you want to head, you'll get lost on the way. You need to set clearly define outcomes of what you want to achieve and what you want your business to look like after you put in the hard work for culture change.

Set clear and measurable goals for the outcomes that you want to achieve from your culture change program. Review the elements of 'FEEL' and determine which outcomes are the ones you want to measure, and set goals and KPIs. Below are a few examples of KPIs:

- Engagement/Satisfaction – Aim for above the engagement benchmark from which ever tool you decided. If it's a satisfaction survey, aim for 80 out of 100 as a starting point.
- Results – Increase customer service satisfaction scores by 10%, increase your net promoter score by six points, improve your profit margin by 20%.
- Innovation – improve system efficiency by 25%, aim for four new ideas per month, implement one big change each month.
- Systems – X number of processes reviewed per month, X number of processes replaced.
- Culture audit – use a tool that provides you with industry benchmarks. Create an ideal culture state, be visual and specific – what does it look like, feel like, sound like, taste like?

Whatever you choose to make your goal, it needs to be meaningful for you. In a health care organization your main KPI of change may be patient outcomes, if you are in manufacturing it may be improving line efficiency, if you are in automotive it may be reduction in labor costs.

This is an important step because if you don't have goals or KPIs then you will not target the areas that you need to target.

Step 2: Current State

Review your current state using a robust and evidence based methodology. There are a number of methods that you can use to measure your culture, depending on the kind of business you are. Don't fall into the trap of thinking engagement/satisfaction surveys will give you the data that you need to change your culture. They are good indicators about some of the outcomes of culture, but they only tell a small part of the story.

The most robust methodology I've experienced is called the Organizational Culture Inventory (OCI) by Human Synergistics. They are an academic organization and therefore their method is extraordinarily well researched. This means you get a good understanding of your current state, however you need to have an Accredited Practitioner to analyze the results and lead you through a change. SynergyIQ have Accredited Practitioners who can help you with this process. I would recommend this tool if you have tried other things and haven't gotten the results you are looking for, and you are able to allocate the necessary budget to the review and the consulting support.

Otherwise, a focus group and self-assessment method is the next best way of discovering your results. This is the method that I regularly use to understand the current state, even if I'm using the OCI product and I back it up with my method below.

Overview of the SynergyIQ Business Assessment Method:
- Organize focus groups – a good rule of thumb is one group of 12-20 people per 150 employees. Selecting a representation of staff sliced horizontally and vertically throughout the business.
- Executive review – review the performance of the executive and run a focus group for them also.
- Start with the FEEL element of the method. This is because people see and feel the impact of culture before they understand the cause.
- Assess the FLOW element to determine what is impacting the FEEL of the business.
- Review the FORM elements to help understand where the problems are originating from. Remembering that leadership expectations and capability sit in FORM. The output from leaders, i.e. communication, management practices, etc. sit in flow, so you may identify concerns that can only be addressed by going to the root cause.

- Desk top review – impartial analysis of the documents of the business, what is written compared to what is done. Strategies, plans, values, processes, website messages, customer communication, customer data, performance data and measures, annual reports, etc.
- One-on-one interviews – clarify information and start to test hypotheses with executives and key managers in individual meetings.

Clear, skilled, and focused facilitation and investigation capability is essential for the focus groups and interviews to enable conversations that address the issues without getting into a whinge-fest.

A big part of understanding your culture environment is assessing what is going to hold you back. Remember the culture you are trying to change is the culture that you are working within.

Resistance is the number one talked about barrier to change. People discuss 'resistors' of change like they are the anti-Christ. In reality resistors are not just people but also elements of your culture, business systems and workforce that will hold you back from changing.

A simple way of assessing the barriers to change in your organization is to do a quick review with your stakeholders. Assessing what is driving change compared to what will be a resistor to change will help you sell the change to others. If you do this activity and find that your resistors far outweigh your drivers, you will struggle to change the environment.

To change anything you must have four things:
- A dissatisfaction with status quo;
- A desire for change;
- Practical steps for change; and
- See value in the change.

If you want to have more success, engage an experienced change manager. Just be aware that some change managers are fantastic at managing a change process for a standard waterfall project, but a culture change program requires a change manager who has the ability to work in a flexible and agile way. There are so many moving parts with culture change that traditional project and change methodologies often fall short.

Step 3 – Analyze Root Cause

Once you have data, both quantitative (e.g. surveys, financials, KPIs) and qualitative (e.g. focus groups, self-assessments, feedback from leaders) you can get down to assessing the gaps and finding the root cause.

This phase is a truly analytical phase and your investigator skills will come into good use. I'm a naturally curious person and love to dig deep into a problem. The reason I focus a lot of attention on this phase is because this is where the gold is discovered. When you dig deep into this phase you will quickly realize what areas you need to focus your attention on. This is the phase that will guide your planning. Without digging into the root cause you will be shooting into the breeze hoping to hit the target.

During this phase, my team and I spend time on the information gathered, including the future state, and determine the largest gaps or the biggest incongruences. When we identify them we start to investigate the root cause.

For example: let's say that the survey data shows low engagement scores, and the focus groups report that people are confused about their roles and don't get feedback.

We would investigate which specific areas in the engagement score are low, potential intention to stay, and review the role confusion, and the way in which people do get feedback.

Generally, you will find in this case that engagement and intention to stay are low because people don't feel that their work or contribution is valued by the business. There may be crossover with their role and another, or perhaps there are a number of people who do exactly the same role and they don't understand the value they add or specific contribution they make. There can be a hundred people in the same role while still being valued for their individual contribution for the role.

This investigation takes some time – don't be tempted to speed through this stage to get to 'action'. You may need to hypothesise first and then find evidence to substantiate the hypothesis. The action you take as a result will have a better chance of success if you truly understand root cause.

Understanding the real reasons for disengagement and role confusion is essential to be able to find solutions. If you assume that feedback is not provided because the performance management system is hard to use, or the leaders are not skilled, then you may miss a critical piece of the puzzle. Perhaps feedback is happening, but it's not helping people see the value of their work. No matter how many times their manager tells them it's valuable, if they don't see value in their work they will be disengaged.

Part of the reason that most change programs fail is because not enough time or effort is spent in this stage.

"Seek first to understand." – Stephen Covey

Step 4 – Plan for Change

Once you have determined the root cause to the problems and the gaps between current and future state, the actions will become obvious. However if you are still at a loss, grab the planning template on the synergyiq.com.au website and create actions under the areas of the model that came up the most during the analysis phase.

	Future	Current	Action
Form			
Flow			
Feel			

Keep it simple so you can focus more time on deployment.

The action that your business requires is determined by the root causes. I'm not going to provide you with a silver bullet here. Although what I will do is list a few areas that appear to be common problems for businesses. These may or may not be the areas or solutions you need so please only use it as a guide and not a solution. The gold is found in step three, don't miss it.

FORM
- Vision – it's not compelling or too wordy and people are unable to connect their work and contribution to it. Solution – write a better vision, get people involved, help them understand how they contribute, be inspiring.
- Values – there are too many and people get confused, the written values are not consistent with the actions of the business, they are too vanilla and don't come alive on a day to day basis. Solution – write values that will help you to achieve your goals, articulate what you expect from the people when they are living the values, help them to translate the values into real life.

- Leadership – expectations of leaders are not clear, management and leadership capabilities are confused, the wrong people are in leadership roles, the leadership behaviors are not articulated. Solution – create a clear understanding of what is expected from leadership, and what is expected of management. Make sure that you are clear about your expectations in both areas – leadership and management. Support and train your leaders to demonstrate the expectations. Move people out of leadership roles if they are not demonstrating and fostering the values.

FLOW
- Systems – they are too slow/complex, the decision-making process is bureaucratic, the customer moments of truth are not understood, the systems of work are hamstrung by power plays. Solution – review the system of work and determine the customer moments of truth, assess where the business production is slow or complicated, find simpler ways, delegate more.
- Processes – they are not facilitating outcomes, they create a bottle neck in customer delivery, they delay an outcome, they don't add value to the customer outcome, they are in place to keep someone in a job. Solution – full process review, determine if they add value to the outcome, if not remove them or create a new process. Hint – don't just do continuous improvement... you can put lipstick on a pig, but it's still a pig. Don't be afraid to remove processes completely – the world won't end... even in safety or government.
- Communication – it's just an information exchange, there is a fear of talking about real issues, collaboration is forced rather than intrinsic, information is top-down or bottom-up only. Solution – understand the power of influence and the way in which people accept information into their minds and hearts. Skill people in the art of giving valuable feedback that is focused on the receiver not the giver. Provide alternative methods of communication and information sharing to support different learning and thinking styles.

- Behavior and Thinking – there's a lack of critical thinking, people are avoiding responsibility, decisions are delayed, collaboration is ineffective, people are not demonstrating values. Solution – expect people to follow the values and behaviors for the company (i.e. manage people in accordance with the expectations), ensure people are clear on expectations by embedding them into all practices, training your people to think critically and educate them on demonstrating the values.

FEEL

- Trust… trust… trust – do I need to say more. Generally trust is broken because of problems in the FLOW and FORM areas of business. Their managers and teams are focused on delivering outcomes at the expense of the relationships and other people at work. Solution – focus on fixing the issues in FORM and FLOW, and then focus on increasing people's interaction with each other in a semi-informal basis. Create environments where people can build relationships themselves. Review your reward systems – what is being rewarded is what is being done. If you reward delivery over collaboration, then you'll get delivery without collaboration.

Create a plan of action that works for your business. Don't make the mistake of looking at what other businesses are doing and think that replicating it in your business will 'fix' your culture. It generally won't. Your business and your people are unique and deserve a bit of thought and analysis, not assumption.

Step 5 – Act

So you have a plan. You've done the research. You've created the interest. Now get on with it. Start action today. Don't wait until it's perfect. Don't wait until you have the perfect framework or strategy. Just get on with changing your culture.

Most organizations don't have the luxury of waiting for months developing change management or leadership capability frameworks or the perfect culture program methodology. Most businesses and business leaders are busy working hard to deliver for the customer. That is why action is so important.

Once you determine an action to take, do it. If your company needs to build leadership capabilities, don't spend weeks or months writing down every capability and debating them. No one will ever agree that 'innovation' is better than 'creativity' and vice versa. Eventually you'll just settle for something anyway, so cut out the middle person and get on with building capabilities. I can tell you right now, that there are no 'leadership' programs out there that will teach your people to be completely awful people. They all teach stock standard capabilities. Absolutely be selective with your provider and your programs. The program should focus not only on the leader, but also their impact on others and the business outcomes. If it's not doing that then it's not worth the investment... but even if you select a mediocre program you can still get benefit if you focus your energy on evaluation and accountability for the skills learned. If you want to know how to select a leadership program that will work for your people head to resources on the SynergyIQ website and you can download a PDF guide which will help.

DON'T BE AFRAID TO EXPERIMENT

Develop your plan, and start acting. Even if it doesn't work, at least you've stepped forward. There is no harm in experimenting, actually it's the best way to find out what works for you. Be realistic about the time frames for change. About 1–2 years before you'll see change in your short-term KPIs, 3–5 years for sustainable change, and 5–10 years for transformative change in a big organization.

Step 6 – Evaluate

All of the steps are important to make sure that your culture change program produces the results that you want. However, I know many great businesses that have completely ignored Steps 1–4 and have still had success. The reason is that they acted, and then they evaluated, they fixed the problems, and then took action again. It's definitely a longer journey than if you plan well, but it's not impossible. The impossible comes when you act, then act, then act, and never stop to check if your actions are having the impact that you want them to have.

You evaluate by reviewing the outcomes from the action you have taken against the goals and KPIs that you have set. Culture, behavior, systems and leadership take time to change, so you may wish to have simple KPIs for the short-term and more robust KPIs that show return on investment in the medium to long term. For example, you won't see a change to the bottom line for at least a year or two, but you will notice an increase in customer satisfaction if your action is directly related to improving customer experience. If you are using a culture diagnosis (like OCI) I recommend two years between measures to see an impact. You'll notice a change in your engagement or satisfaction surveys first so use them as your short-term indicators that your actions are getting traction. Just be aware that these short term KPIs will go up and down before sustainable change occurs.

This is a good opportunity to not only review the actions that you have taken, but also to review the KPIs and goals that you have set. As the business matures through the transition they move from engagement/satisfaction surveys to culture and business effectiveness diagnosis so that they can dig deeper into the causation factors and levers for change.

Don't be afraid to stop doing something if it's having no impact at all. Strategically stop I mean. A strategic stop happens after a proper review against KPIs and outcomes determines that even after putting in the right kind of effort (including holding people accountable for change) the program is not able to deliver the outcomes required. It's not a reaction to yours or someone's opinion of the activity.

Step 7 – Go Back to the Start and Do it All Again Until You Get the Results You Are Looking For

I think this step speaks for itself. Change doesn't just happen because you want it to. Change happens through deliberate and consistent action. Action that is planned, tested and evaluated. If you are struggling to get the change that you want then it's time to call in an expert to help you diagnose the problems and find sustainable solutions.

Killers of Culture Change

There's actually a Step 8, well it's not really a Step, it's a basic principle.... Enjoy it. Yep, that's actually possible.

Change can be enjoyable when it's done well. Yes, there is effort involved and yes, there is hard work, and yes, there is know-how needed. But try not to make it into a desperate dash and something harder than it is. A number of great programs have been killed because of a few key people sabotaging the program.

Below is a list of culture program killers to be aware of:

1. The Superhero – "Here I come to save the day! Here is a big shiny object that will impress and confuse you, and of course, only I know how to implement it." If your program is a one-man show, and isn't well researched and collaborative, it's dead.

2. The Dystopian World – "It's too hard/big/complex/long…" How do you eat an elephant? One small bite at a time. Yep, the metaphor is gross but you get the picture. Don't catastrophize; just take one action at a time.

3. The Vanilla Effect – "Here's the off-the-shelf program that everyone is doing." If you aren't experimenting and trying different things then you'll end up with an uncreative and dull program that everyone yawns at. If it's boring, it's dead.

4. The Shooting Yourself in the Foot Approach – "We should change the way we do that, we should get our leaders coaching, we should give our customers more…" Without taking action, you can 'should and hope' for change all you want, but nothing is going to change. Get on with it.

5. The Action Distraction – "Let's try this, and this, and this, and this. Oh and why aren't you doing anything, do this!" Doing more and more, is not culture change. Sometimes culture change is not visual and happens behind the scenes. Don't fall in the trap of constant action – pick something and go deep with it, or you'll run out of steam before the last act.

6. The Premature Evacuation – "Let's do culture change…" Two months later… "We've done culture now, let's do something else." Culture is enduring, and a culture transformation program may take years to make the change you need for your business.

Don't fall in the trap of thinking a six month effort or training program is all you need to do. This is a long term undertaking. Think Kamasutra not Wham Bam.

Key Take-away

If you don't plan for success; plan for failure.

Self-coaching Questions

- How have I planned in the past?
- How often do we act without reviewing the results?
- How can we change this approach? How can we dig deeper into understanding our current situation?
- What support do we need to make this transformation a success?

Author's Final Word
What Now?

> "Train people well enough so they can leave, treat them well enough so they don't want to. If you look after your staff they will look after your customers. It's that simple."
>
> Richard Branson

Author's Final Word: What Now?

The best thing that I can leave you with is this advice… culture is not complex, it's not hard to change, and it's not something that someone else does.

Culture just is. It's the way the business forms, flows and feels.

Culture transformation takes time, effort and know-how.

You now have the know-how from reading this book. There's really no more magic to it. People will try and baffle you and start talking to you about mindset, deep values, change management processes, frameworks and data sets, which are all a part of an integrated system of transformation. But honestly… just start looking at better ways of doing business. If you can keep your focus on creating efficiency, effectiveness and great customer outcomes… instead of process, fear and what you don't know… you'll move in the right direction. PS get help when you need it. There is no shame in saying, "Help me make my business better."

You'll be amazed at how quickly values are lived, mindsets are changed, and change happens when you focus your attention on making the business a better place to work and do business with.

Let the way the business feels inspire your transformation, and act. Start with you, then the foundation stones (FORM), then systems and practices (FLOW), and the way people FEEL about the business will fix itself.

You have the ability, and now the know-how, to create a business that delivers results and that people love.

All the best, culture warrior!

Michelle

About the Author

Michelle is an author, entrepreneur, coach and business consultant.

Leveraging her interest in people and business development, she traded in her accounting career to pursue her undergraduate and graduate degrees in human behavior, organizational development and ethics. Having held a range of positions in human resources and senior management, Michelle is proud of her successes. Among other accomplishments, she is particularly proud of the leadership programs, workforce planning methodologies, and business transformation strategies that she has created and implemented.

In 2013, Michelle started a boutique business consultancy where she specializes in leadership development, business strategy, and culture transformation. In 2016, along with her partner, she launched an online platform that is revolutionizing the music education sector. The platform manages administration functions so the educator can focus on teaching and finding new clients, through the system.

Throughout her career, Michelle has worked with many organizations including Anglicare, ShineSA, RenewalSA, SA Water, RSB, Dan Murphy's, Novatech Creative Event Technology, the City of Charles Sturt, the City of Salisbury, City of Greater Bendigo, Helping Hand Aged Care, the University of South Australia, the National Trust of SA, Meals on Wheels and BusinessSA, to name a few.

As a keynote and guest speaker, she has spoken at conferences and live events across Australia. Her speaking topics include leadership, business culture, resilience and personal leadership branding.

An accredited leadership coach and culture profiler, Michelle's professional associations include Human Synergystics, Hermann International (HBDI), Australian Human Resource Institute (AHRI), the South Australia Writers Centre, and the Leaders Institute of South Australia. Michelle also volunteers as a mentor for young entrepreneurs and young business professionals.

She has traveled and worked throughout Australia, Canada, the United States, England, Scotland, France, the United Arab Emirates, Egypt, Jordan, Malaysia, Thailand, Borneo, Singapore, Bali, Fiji and New Caledonia.

Michelle T Holland is the author of *Energy Vampires Suck*, *Unearthing Vampires* and *Culture Inc.*, and lives in South Australia with her two children, her partner, two adorable dogs… and a rabbit.

Recommended
Resources

Recommended Resources

Conference Speaker

Keynotes, masterclasses, and engaging presentations.

Michelle is a member of the new generation of speakers and authors who give generously to their audience and maintain relevance through continual research and development. Each presentation is a bit different, because as Michelle learns and grows, so does her ability to provide a unique look at the world through the creative and curious eyes of a corporate problem solver. Michelle enables her audiences to think creatively and act differently to create better businesses.

She will provide your audience with information, resources and direction that enables them to lead a transformation either within their business, or themselves. Her favorite topics are business culture, transformational leadership and leading transformation.

"Michelle is personable and approachable and a pleasure to work with. She found time for all the delegates that approached her for further information at the event. I cannot recommend her enough. The expertise she brought to the event was invaluable to everyone in attendance!" Doug Power, Event Manager IQPC

"Our participants left Michelle's presentation with a renewed sense of energy which was fantastic given it was the after lunch session! I'm pleased to recommend Michelle as a spear who engages and educates." Taryn Sexton, CEO LG Professionals

SynergyIQ's Culture, Leadership and Business Diagnostic Tools

Find out more about the online SynergyIQ Culture Transformation Action Planner, SynergyIQ Culture Archetypes Profiler and other business diagnostic tools at your disposal.

Discover how your culture is contributing to or holding you back from the success that you want. Profile your current employees using the online tool to assess their fit within the culture you are trying to create.

Go to synergyiq.com.au to learn more.

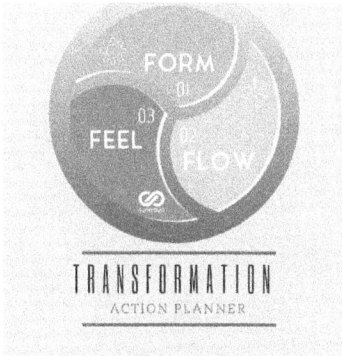

Transformation Action Planner using 3Fs methodology

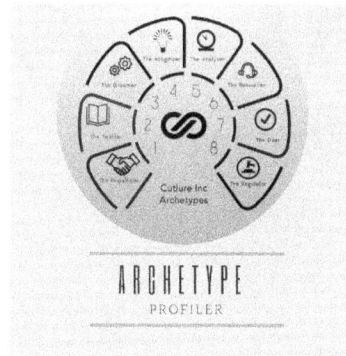

Culture Archetypes Profiler

References

References

- Aguirre, D., von Post, R., and Alpern, M. (2013), *Culture's Role in Enabling Organizational Change*, Booz & Company.

- Brown, S. L., and Vaughan, C. C. (2009). *Play: How it shapes the brain, opens the imagination, and invigorates the soul.* Avery.

- Catmull, E. E., and Wallace, A. (2014) *Creativity, Inc.: Overcoming the Unseen Forces That Stand in the Way of True Inspiration*, Random House.

- Collins, J. C. (2001). *Good to Great: why some companies make the leap ... and others don't*, Harper Business.

- Covey, S. R. (1989) *The 7 Habits of Highly Effective People: Restoring the Character Ethic*, Harper Collins

- Damasio, A. R. (2000) *Descartes'* Error: Emotion, Reason, and the Human Brain, Quill.

- Ewenstein, B., Smith, W., and Sologar, A. (2015), *Changing Change Management*, McKinsey and Company.

- Fleishman, E. A. and Harris, E. F. (1962), Patterns of Leadership Behavior Related to Employee Grievances and Turnover. *Personnel Psychology*, 15: 43–56. doi:10.1111/j.1744-6570.1962.tb01845.x

- Frankl, V. E. (1946/1984). *Man's Search for Meaning: An introduction to logotherapy*, Simon & Schuster.

- Freakonomics (2018), 'What Uber can teach us about gender pay gap', NPR Freakonomics Podcast, 7 February 2018.

- Hari, J. (2018). *Lost connections: Uncovering the real causes of depression-- and the unexpected solutions*, Bloomsbury.

- Henderson, M. (2014), *Above the Line: How to Create a Company Culture that Engages Employees, Delights Customers and Delivers Results*, Wiley.

- Holland, M. T. (2016), *Energy Vampire Suck: A story about discovering your inner strength and taking back your life*, ETI.

- Hsieh, T. (2010) *Delivering Happiness: a path to profits, passion, and purpose*, Business Plus

- Human Synergistics (2016), 'Why culture and leadership matter': research and development by Cooke, R. A. and J Clayton Lafferty, J. C., Human Synergistics International.

- Maslow, A. H. (1943), A Theory of Human Motivation *Psychological Review*, 55(4), 430–437.

- Morrison, General D. (2013), Chief of Army Lieutenant General David Morrison message about unacceptable behavior, https://youtu.be/QaqpoeVgr8U

- Popli, S. and Rizvi, I. A. (2017). Leadership style and service orientation: The catalytic role of employee engagement, *Journal of Service Theory and Practice*, 27(1), 292–310.

- Sandberg, S, and Grant, A. (2017) *Option B: Facing Adversity, Building Resilience, and Finding Joy*, Random House

- Sinek, S. (2009). *Start With Why: How great leaders inspire everyone to take action*, Portfolio

- Sinek, S. (2014) *Leaders Eat Last: Why Some Teams Pull Together and Others Don't*, Portfolio/Penguin.

- Yafang, T (2014) Relationship Between Organizational Culture, Leadership Behavior and Job Satisfaction, *BMC Health Serv Res* 11(98) doi: 10.1186/1472-6963-11-98 PMCID: PMC3123547